Smarter Than Yesterday

One Step at a Time

Darren Gibbons & Alex Knowles

Acknowledgements

This book was not created in isolation. It grew from countless conversations, shared miles, quiet reflections and the encouragement of people who kept us moving forward.

To the athletes we've coached and trained alongside — this book belongs as much to you as to us. Every breakthrough, every setback, every story of resilience has shaped the words you now hold. You've shown us again and again what courage, discipline and persistence look like in real life.

To our wider community at Smart Performance Coaching — thank you for showing up, pushing harder and proving that progress is contagious. Your dedication inspired us to create not just a book, but a resource that feels like a coach and a teammate on every page.

And to you, the reacer — thank you for choosing to commit your time and focus to this journey. Books only come alive when they are lived through. Every page you complete, every reflection you write, every action you take is proof that change is possible.

Our hope is simple: that these 365 days help you keep moving — one step, one choice, one day at a time. May you finish each page and each day, smarter than yesterday.

Table of Contents

January — Beginnings 16
February — Steadiness 38
March — Renewal 57
April — Momentum 78
May — Endurance 99
June — Reflection 120
July — Courage 140
August — Resilience 161
September — Focus 182
October — Depth 202
November — Gratitude 223
December — Legacy 244

Introduction

A year is not defined by a single decision but by a series of moments. Every sunrise gives you another chance to step forward, another chance to realign with who you want to become. The truth is, change rarely happens in grand leaps. It happens in ordinary days, repeated choices and the quiet courage to continue when no one is watching.

Think about it: a single moment of inspiration may spark a beginning, but it is the steady rhythm of small actions that carries you through the days, weeks and months ahead. You don't become healthier in one workout. You don't become wiser in one reflection. You don't transform your mindset in a single flash of clarity. Growth is always the product of accumulation—tiny pieces stacking until they form something solid.

This book is designed to walk with you through 365 of those days. Not by overwhelming you with long lectures or impossible demands, but by offering daily seeds of thought and action. Seeds are small, often overlooked, but they hold immense potential. When planted, watered and given light, they grow into something far greater than their beginnings. That's what these daily entries are meant to be—seeds. What they become will depend on your willingness to tend to them.

You don't need to know the full blueprint before you begin. Seeds don't demand certainty; they demand attention. In the same way, these pages are not about controlling your entire year from day one, but about showing up daily with openness and persistence. The process itself will shape you.

The Power of Small Moments

A common trap in self-growth is waiting for the perfect time—the big decision, the flawless plan, the total reset. But perfection is an illusion. Progress begins when you use the moments you already have. That's why this book focuses on the small, the daily, the repeatable.

Consider how easily a day can slip by unnoticed. You wake, move through tasks, handle responsibilities and collapse into bed—only to wonder where the hours went. Without attention, days blur. But with awareness, each day can become a chance to practice presence. Reading a short reflection, answering one honest question and taking one simple action may not seem like much. Yet over time, those minutes compound into transformation.

The beauty of small moments is that they're available to everyone. You don't need wealth, status, or perfect conditions. You don't need to wait until you feel ready. You simply begin where you are, with what you have.

Short by Design

Each day in these pages is intentionally short. The words are meant to be read in a few minutes, but the reflections are designed to stay with you for hours. Think of them as sparks: a quick flame that lights the deeper work of your own thoughts and actions.

Why short? Because depth doesn't require length. A single sentence, if it lands at the right time, can shift perspective more than an entire chapter of theory. Brevity makes these ideas usable. You can read them at the breakfast table, in a quiet pause at work, or before you sleep. No excuses about time.

But don't mistake short for shallow. The entries are compact so they can travel with you, echoing in the back of your mind as the day unfolds. They are meant to be lived with, not just read and forgotten.

Equipped, Not Impressed

The goal of this book isn't to impress you with lofty language or complex theories. It's to equip you. Tools are more valuable than speeches. A hammer in hand is worth more than a lecture about architecture. In the same way, a practical prompt that shifts your perspective today is worth more than pages of philosophy that gather dust.

Equipping means giving you something you can actually use: a thought to consider, a question to wrestle with, a challenge to attempt. These are the building blocks of change. You won't remember every word in these pages, but you don't need to. What matters is the action they spark.

The Myth of the Perfect Life

One of the biggest lies we tell ourselves is that progress requires a perfect schedule or a quiet life. We imagine that once work slows down, or once family demands ease, or once the calendar clears, then we'll finally be able to focus. But life never fully clears. There will always be noise, interruptions, fatigue and surprise.

You don't need perfection to grow. You need presence. You don't need every hour of your day—just a few intentional minutes. Even in the busiest seasons, a small pause is possible. And those pauses matter more than you think. A single breath of awareness can prevent an entire day of distraction. A five-minute action can reinforce an identity you want to build.

Stop waiting for the perfect conditions. Start with the conditions you have. The real work of growth happens not in ideal circumstances but in real ones—messy, crowded, unpredictable. That's where your strength is built.

A Clear Focus, a Simple Step

So what do you need to make progress? Not more information. Not more time. Not more perfection. You need clarity and action. A clear focus on what matters and a simple step to move you forward.

Clarity keeps you from scattering your energy across dozens of half-commitments. Action prevents you from getting stuck in endless reflection. Together, they create momentum.

That's why every entry in this book follows the same rhythm: **read, reflect, act.** You'll encounter an Insight to sharpen focus, a Question to spark honest reflection and a Micro Challenge to move you forward. Small, deliberate, repeatable.

The Willingness to Return

Finally, the most important ingredient: the willingness to return tomorrow.

Consistency is the difference between wishing and becoming. Anyone can start with excitement. Few continue with persistence. But if you choose to return each day—to read, to reflect, to act—you will see change. Not instantly, but inevitably.

Some days you'll miss. That's normal. The key is not to let one missed day turn into ten. Return without guilt. Start again without drama. Progress is not about never slipping; it's about always returning.

The year ahead will not be perfect. You won't meet every challenge flawlessly. But if you keep showing up, you will grow. You will accumulate strength, awareness and resilience. Step by step, you will become someone who trusts their own consistency more than their moods. And that is where true transformation begins.

Closing Thought

A year is not built in a single decision. It is built in thousands of moments—moments where you choose presence over autopilot, progress over perfection, courage over fear. Every sunrise is another chance. Every page in this book is another seed.

Plant them. Water them. Return tomorrow. Over time, you will see what grows.

1. **The Insight** – a brief reflection to spark thought. It introduces a theme for the day and offers a lens to see your choices differently.
2. **The Question** – a prompt to help you turn reflection inward. Growth begins with honest self-awareness and a good question can do more than a long explanation.
3. **The Micro Challenge** – one small action to practice that day. Growth doesn't come from theory but from action. These challenges are designed to be practical, simple and achievable. Done daily, they will reshape your year.

Think of this as a rhythm: read, reflect, act.

The Categories

The book is organised around themes that repeat throughout the year. Each category highlights a different strength that contributes to a meaningful life. Together, they keep your growth balanced.

- **Courage** – Fear will always whisper "stay safe." Courage is choosing to act anyway to risk honesty, vulnerability, or change.

- **Resilience** – Life will knock you down. Resilience is the ability to rise again, to keep moving forward with wisdom gained from the struggle.

- **Discipline** – The backbone of progress. Discipline is about showing up, even when you don't feel like it. It's the daily decisions that add up to identity.

- **Energy** – Your energy is your fuel. Protecting, renewing and directing it wisely makes everything else possible.

- **Relationships** – Connection is at the heart of a full life. Relationships thrive on presence, consistency and care.

- **Empathy** – More than agreement, empathy is about listening, understanding and creating safety for others to be real.

- **Boundaries** – Saying no where you must so you can say yes where it matters. Boundaries protect your time, energy and values.

- **Curiosity** – The drive to ask, learn and explore. Curiosity expands horizons and strengthens relationships.

- **Gratitude** – The practice of noticing what is already good. Gratitude turns ordinary days into meaningful ones.

- **Grit** – The quiet strength to keep going when motivation fades. Grit outlasts obstacles and proves endurance.
- **Perspective** – The ability to step back and see the bigger picture. Perspective balances hardship with hope.
- **Growth** – The process of stretching beyond comfort and becoming more than you were yesterday.
- **Reflection** – The pause that turns experience into wisdom. Reflection prevents wasted lessons.
- **Focus** – The discipline of directing attention where it matters most. Focus cuts clutter and builds momentum.

How to Use This Book

There's no single right way to read these pages. This book is designed to walk with you for a year, but you can also treat it as a well you return to whenever you need strength, clarity, or encouragement.

Each entry has three parts:

1. **The Insight** – a short reflection that frames the theme for the day.
2. **The Question** – a prompt to help you pause and apply it to your own life.
3. **The Micro Challenge** – one small action you can try right away.

Here are some ways to use it:

- **Daily** – Read one entry each morning or evening, let the question sit with you and take on the micro challenge.
- **In the moment** – Flip to any page when you need focus, encouragement, or a spark of perspective. Trust that the page you land on will meet you where you are.
- **In blocks** – Read a week or month at a time, noticing how themes connect and build on each other.
- **As a journal companion** – Use the daily questions as prompts for journaling or reflection.

Some days you'll want to move slowly, rereading and reflecting. Other days you may want to scan quickly or skip ahead. Both are fine. The value isn't in strict order but in steady use. The more consistently you return to these pages, the more they will shape the way you see, think and act.

This book is meant to be lived with, not just read. Carry it, mark it, return to it. Let it challenge you, encourage you and remind you that growth is built in small, daily steps

January — Beginnings

January is the clean slate, the open door, the quiet signal that something new has started. It carries the energy of fresh starts, but also the weight of choice. Every beginning is filled with possibility and how you step into it matters. This month is about foundations—building habits, clarifying direction and shaping routines that will carry you further than a single burst of motivation ever could.

Beginnings are fragile. They ask for gentleness as well as determination. The temptation is to start too fast, to burn brightly and then fade. Resist the urge to overhaul everything in a rush. Beginnings are strongest when they're steady. This month, focus on consistency rather than perfection. You don't have to do everything at once; you only need to do something every day.

Think small and specific: ten minutes of movement, a full glass of water, one page of notes, three quiet breaths before you open your inbox. Lay bricks, not bonfires. Track what you repeat, not what you promise. If you miss a day, step back in without drama. Progress loves calm company.

Over the next 31 days, you'll be invited to practice discipline, courage, gratitude and reflection. Some entries will feel effortless; others will press against resistance. That's the point. Growth isn't about comfort—it's about stretching past what's familiar, learning what holds you back and building the strength to keep going anyway.

Treat January as a slow, steady build. Plant the seeds of the habits you want to see flourish. Protect your mornings, tidy your evenings and leave room for recovery. Trust that the momentum you begin now will carry into the months ahead. Every page, every repetition, every small promise kept is a step forward.

If you want a nudge, try this simple frame each day: one thing to move your body, one thing to feed your mind, one thing to clear your space. Then, one sentence about what you're proud of. Keep it light. Keep it doable. Keep showing up.

The only requirement is that you begin—and then begin again tomorrow. Start where you are, with what you have and let January be the month you quietly become the person who follows through.

Day 1: Every Beginning Matters

This is where it begins. Starting is an act of courage in itself, because it means you've decided to stop waiting. This year will bring insights, challenges and growth, but none of it matters without today. Beginning is proof that you are willing to show up for yourself.

→ What does starting this adventure mean to you right now?
Micro Challenge: Write one sentence about why you are beginning this journey. Keep it somewhere visible to remind you on the harder days ahead.

Day 2: Courage Starts Small

Courage:
Courage isn't always a grand leap — sometimes it's a small step forward. Speaking up, asking for help, or trying something new counts as bravery. Every small act builds strength for bigger challenges. Waiting to feel fearless only delays growth. Courage grows when you act despite fear. Even tiny steps are proof of bravery.

→ Where can you show small courage today?
Micro Challenge: Do one action you've been avoiding, even if it feels uncomfortable.

Day 3: Failure Is Feedback

Resilience:
Setbacks are not the end; they are information. Resilience means using failure as fuel, as feedback that sharpens your next attempt. Each stumble is proof that you're moving and proof that you're learning.

→ **How can you use your last setback as a lesson?**
Micro Challenge:
Write down one thing you learned from a recent mistake. Apply it today.

Day 4: The Power of Starting

Discipline:
Discipline isn't punishment — it's alignment. Every small promise you keep points your life in a clearer direction. When you act on priorities instead of impulses, your days stop happening to you and start working for you. Motivation comes and goes; discipline decides anyway. The calendar is where your values either show up or disappear.

→ **Where does your day need alignment with your priorities?**
Micro Challenge: Block 20 minutes for one priority and complete it start to finish without switching tasks.

Day 5: Energy is Protection

Energy:
Your energy is limited — guard it carefully. Every distraction, demand, or worry takes a portion of it. Protecting energy means choosing wisely where to spend it. When your energy is guarded, you can give your best where it matters most. A recharged you is a stronger you. Energy fuels everything else.

→ **Where are you leaking energy unnecessarily?**
Micro Challenge: Remove one drain from your day and take a short rest.

Day 6: Small Acts, Strong Bonds

Relationships:
Strong relationships are built in ordinary moments. Small acts of kindness, attention and care add up over time. Waiting for the "big moment" misses the daily chances to connect. Consistency matters more than intensity. Relationships thrive on small, steady signals of care. Trust is built moment by moment.

→ **Who could use a small sign of care today?**
Micro Challenge: Send one quick message of appreciation or encouragement.

Day 7: Empathy Sees Deeper

Empathy:
Actions are often just the surface of a deeper story. Empathy invites you to pause judgment and wonder what's underneath. Understanding doesn't excuse harm, but it humanises the human. Seeing someone's context softens conflict and builds compassion. Empathy is the bridge from distance to connection. It starts with choosing to see deeper.

→ **Who needs your empathy today?**
Micro Challenge: Imagine three possible pressures someone may be facing before you respond.

Day 8: Boundaries Guard Freedom

Boundaries:
Boundaries aren't walls — they're gates. They protect your priorities, time and peace. Without them, you give everything away and end up drained. With them, you create space to live and work with intention. Boundaries make freedom possible by defining limits. Clarity brings strength.

→ **What boundary would protect your freedom today?**
Micro Challenge: Say no once today, clearly and kindly.

Day 9: Curiosity Sparks Growth

Curiosity:
Curiosity is the antidote to stagnation. It asks, "What else is possible?" and opens doors where walls once stood. Growth begins when you step into questions instead of clinging to answers. Wonder keeps your discovery in small, daily ways. Every question is a doorway.

→ **What question could spark growth today?**
Micro Challenge: Ask one new "what if" about a routine task.

Day 10: Gratitude Shifts Perspective

Gratitude:
Gratitude doesn't erase problems but reframes them. By naming what's good, you create balance against what's hard. Gratitude turns scarcity into sufficiency. Even in challenge, something steady remains to be thankful for. A grateful heart softens fear and strengthens endurance. Gratitude is perspective in action.

→ **What's one thing you can thank today?**
Micro Challenge: Write down three small blessings before bed.

Day 11: Grit Keeps Going

Grit:
Excitement may start a journey, but grit finishes it. Grit is the stubborn decision to keep moving, even when motivation fades. It is built in the boring middle, not the thrilling beginning. Each act of perseverance strengthens your ability to last. Over time, grit outpaces talent and luck. Grit is staying power.

→ **Where do you need grit today?**
Micro Challenge: Work five minutes longer on a task you want to quit.

Day 12: Perspective Brings Peace

Perspective:
When problems fill your view, they feel overwhelming. Perspective zooms out and reminds you of the bigger picture. Most struggles are smaller in scale than they appear in the moment. Stepping back brings calm and clarity. With perspective, peace returns. Vision changes weight.

→ **How could perspective lighten your problem today?**
Micro Challenge: Write one sentence that frames your challenge as temporary.

Day 13: Growth Demands Stretch

Growth:
Growth rarely feels comfortable. Stretch is the sign that you're moving into new territory. Each small step outside your comfort zone expands what you're capable of. What feels uncomfortable today becomes normal tomorrow. Over time, stretch transforms into strength. Growth is born in discomfort.

→ **Where could you stretch yourself today?**
Micro Challenge: Do one task that feels slightly uncomfortable.

Day 14: Reflection Reveals Lessons

Reflection:
Without reflection, life becomes a blur of repeated mistakes. Pausing allows you to see patterns and learn from them. Reflection transforms failure into teaching and success into guidance. Every lesson strengthens your path forward. Reflection makes experience meaningful. The past becomes wisdom through reflection.

→ **What lesson is waiting to be noticed?**
Micro Challenge: Write down one insight from your week and how you'll apply it.

Day 15: Focus Shapes Progress

Focus:
Progress isn't about speed but direction. Focus shapes where your energy goes and what grows as a result. Scattered attention leads to motion without results. Concentrated focus multiplies effectiveness. Your progress will always follow your attention. Focus creates the path forward.

→ **What deserves your focus today?**
Micro Challenge: Choose one priority and protect 30 minutes for it.

Day 16: Courage Faces Fear

Courage:
Fear whispers reasons to wait, but courage steps forward anyway. Bravery isn't the absence of fear; it's action in spite of it. Each time you confront fear, its power shrinks. Courage doesn't demand perfection — just a single step. Fear fades when faced. Courage frees you to live boldly.

→ **What fear could you face today?**
Micro Challenge: Do one action you've been avoiding because of fear.

Day 17: Resilience Chooses Patience

Resilience:
Not every challenge can be solved quickly. Resilience is the patience to endure when progress is slow. Waiting without giving up is its own strength. Patience protects your energy while time does its work. Every moment of waiting well builds character and calm. Resilience grows in the pauses.

→ **Where could patience help you endure today?**
Micro Challenge: Take three slow breaths before reacting to something frustrating.

Day 18: Discipline Creates Freedom

Discipline:
At first, discipline feels restrictive. But over time, it frees you from chaos and regret. When you act consistently, you don't waste energy on constant decisions. Discipline creates routines that support your best self. Freedom comes when you're no longer ruled by impulse. Discipline is structure that liberates.

→ **Where could discipline create freedom today?**
Micro Challenge: Stick to one routine action without compromise.

Day 19: Energy is Created Through Action

Energy:
Energy doesn't only drain — it can also grow. Moving your body, pursuing purpose, or connecting with others can fuel you. Waiting until you "feel like it" often keeps you stuck. Action itself generates momentum and energy. The more you engage, the more energy flows. Energy is made, not just spent.

→ **What action could create energy for you today?**
Micro Challenge: Do one short burst of movement or connection.

Day 20: Presence Strengthens Relationships

Relationships:
Relationships thrive on presence. Being fully with someone, without distraction, communicates value. Presence is rare in a world of divided attention. Even short, focused moments build trust and connection. You don't need hours — you need honesty and attention. Presence is proof of care.

→ **Who deserves your full attention today?**
Micro Challenge: Put your phone aside for one conversation and listen deeply.

Day 21: Empathy Opens Doors

Empathy:
Walls rise quickly when people feel misunderstood. Empathy lowers those walls by saying, "I hear you." Understanding doesn't require agreement, but it creates connection. Empathy often softens what argument hardens. Listening with compassion opens doors for resolution. Connection begins with seeing through another's eyes.

→ **Who needs to feel heard today?**
Micro Challenge: Reflect back what someone says before giving your own opinion.

Day 22: Boundaries Protect Peace

Boundaries:
Without boundaries, stress and noise creep into every corner of life. Peace requires clear limits on what enters your time and mind. Boundaries are not rejection but protection. They allow you to preserve what matters most. Peace is defended, not discovered. Boundaries keep it safe.

→ **What boundary could protect your peace today?**
Micro Challenge: Turn off one channel of noise for the rest of the day.

Day 23: Curiosity Deepens Connection

Curiosity:
Curiosity isn't only for learning — it strengthens relationships too. Asking thoughtful questions shows care and interest. People open up when they feel truly seen. Curiosity replaces assumption with understanding. It turns conversations into connections. Relationships grow through genuine curiosity.

→ **Who could you get curious about today?**
Micro Challenge: Ask one person a question you've never asked before.

Day 24: Gratitude Multiplies Enough

Gratitude:
Comparison shrinks joy; gratitude expands it. When you count what you already have, the sense of enough grows. Gratitude doesn't ignore what's missing — it balances it. The more you notice blessings, the richer life feels. Enough is not a number, but a perspective. Gratitude multiplies enough.

→ **What do you already have more than enough of?**
Micro Challenge: Write down three things you wouldn't trade for anything.

Day 25: Grit Pushes One Step More

Grit:
Progress often hides just beyond the point of quitting. Grit is the decision to go one step further. It doesn't require perfection — only persistence. Each extra effort builds endurance and self-belief. Over time, grit is what turns effort into achievement. Stay with it longer than your doubt.

→ **Where could you push one step more today?**
Micro Challenge: Work five minutes beyond your urge to stop.

Day 26: Perspective Reframes Challenges

Perspective:
The story you tell about your challenge shapes how you experience it. Seeing it as training instead of punishment changes its weight. Perspective doesn't erase pain, but it transforms it into purpose. A wider view reveals opportunity in struggle. Your lens shapes your load.

→ **How could you reframe your current challenge?**
Micro Challenge: Write one sentence framing your struggle as training.

Day 27: Growth is a Daily Choice

Growth:
Growth isn't automatic — it's chosen. Each day you can stay comfortable or step into stretch. Small risks, repeated, expand your capacity over time. What feels hard today becomes easier tomorrow. Growth accumulates in daily decisions. Choosing growth is choosing your future.

→ **What small choice could grow you today?**
Micro Challenge: Do one task you've been postponing out of discomfort.

Day 28: Reflection Builds Direction

Reflection:
Life without reflection drifts aimlessly. Pausing allows you to ask where you're heading and why. Reflection turns activity into purpose. It saves you from chasing everything and missing what matters. With reflection, each step gains direction. Clarity grows in stillness.

→ **Where could reflection guide you today?**
Micro Challenge: Write down your top three priorities for this week.

Day 29: Focus Simplifies Decisions

Focus:
When everything feels equal, decision-making overwhelms you. Focus simplifies by naming what matters most. Once the priority is clear, choices become easier. Focus turns clutter into clarity. Simplicity follows attention. The clearer the focus, the lighter the load.

→ **What one priority could simplify your decisions today?**
Micro Challenge: Choose one goal and let it guide today's choices.

Day 30: Courage Means Beginning

Courage:
Starting is often the hardest part. Fear and doubt delay action, but courage chooses to begin anyway. The first step doesn't have to be big — it just has to be taken. Beginning creates momentum where hesitation creates stagnation. Courage is built by beginnings. Every start is a victory.

→ **What beginning are you delaying?**
Micro Challenge: Take the first step today, however small.

Day 31: Resilience Finds Strength in Struggle

Resilience:
Struggles are not signs of weakness but training for strength. Each challenge builds endurance for future battles. Resilience grows when you choose to see struggle as shaping you. Pressure can crush you or strengthen you — perspective decides. With resilience, hardship becomes growth in disguise. Strength is forged in fire.

→ **What struggle is shaping your strength today?**
Micro Challenge: Write one way your current challenge could make you stronger.

January Workbook – Foundations

Beginnings matter. The habits you establish in these first weeks will shape how you grow through the rest of the year. Think of January as your foundation stone. A strong base makes everything built on top of it stronger. Use this page to pause, reflect and set intentions that give you stability for the months ahead.

1. Reflection

What did I do this month that I'm most proud of?

_____
_____
_____

What new habits did I try? Which ones felt natural? Which felt forced?

_____
_____
_____

Where did I already see a difference in my energy, mindset, or results?

_____
_____
_____

What challenges made it hard to stay consistent?

_____
_____
_____

What do I want to carry forward into February?

_____
_____
_____

2. Journaling Prompt

Write a short mission statement for this year. Imagine it's a compass you can return to whenever you feel lost. Keep it simple and strong. Example: 'This year I will choose discipline over comfort, growth over ease and progress over perfection.'

_____
_____
_____

3. Exercise

Draw a three-level pyramid.
- Bottom layer: Write your 3 most important values.
- Middle layer: List the habits that support them.
- Top layer: Write the result you want to aim for this year.

[Use the space below to draw, sketch, or note your ideas.]

_____
_____
_____

February — Steadiness

The first rush of the year fades quickly. By February, the buzz of beginnings has quieted and what remains is the reality of routine. The mornings are darker, the days shorter and the temptation to quit is real. This is the month where enthusiasm fades and the habits you planted in January are tested.

February's invitation is simple: stay steady. Steadiness doesn't mean perfection and it doesn't mean speed. It means showing up, even when you'd rather not. It means honouring the commitments you made when your energy was high, even when your energy dips. Every small act of consistency builds trust with yourself and that trust is the foundation of resilience.

This is also the month where love takes its place — not only the love celebrated on Valentine's Day, but love for the process itself. Love for growth, love for the people who cheer you on and love for the version of yourself that is still becoming. To keep going requires loyalty — to your vision, your values and your future self. Love is the quiet fuel of endurance.

Expect resistance here. Progress will sometimes feel slower. The spark that carried you through January may dim and that's normal. Growth is not always exciting; sometimes it's repetitive, even dull. But those are the very moments where strength is built. Each time you keep going, you prove to yourself that you can.

Steadiness is what transforms goals into realities. Without it, momentum stalls. With it, even the smallest habits add up to something extraordinary. February's challenge is to hold your ground, to keep walking and to trust that every step forward is shaping you in ways you may not yet see.

This month, stay steady. The progress you protect now becomes the progress you'll celebrate later.

Day 32: Discipline Honors Identity

Discipline:
Who you are is revealed by what you repeatedly do. Discipline turns values into visible habits. Each consistent act strengthens identity and integrity. Skipping discipline erodes trust in yourself, while keeping it builds confidence. Discipline aligns your life with who you want to be. Your habits write your story.

→ **What habit reflects your identity today?**
Micro Challenge: Choose one action that matches your values and complete it.

Day 33: Energy Needs Renewal

Energy:
You can't run endlessly without rest. Energy is renewed by rhythm — work, rest and recovery. Ignoring this cycle leads to burnout but honouring it builds endurance. Renewal isn't indulgence; it's preparation for strength. Choosing rest wisely creates more capacity tomorrow. Energy grows in the pause.

→ **Where do you need renewal today?**
Micro Challenge: Schedule 15 minutes of deliberate rest.

Day 34: Relationships Thrive on Consistency

Relationships:
Grand gestures may impress, but consistency builds trust. Steady care, regular presence and reliable support matter most. People remember how you show up daily, not occasionally. Relationships grow strong through repeated signals of value. Consistency is love in action.

→ **Who could you show up for today?**
Micro Challenge: Send one simple check-in to someone important.

Day 35: Empathy Strengthens Leadership

Empathy:
True leadership is built on empathy. People don't just follow your vision — they follow how you make them feel. Empathy connects authority with humanity. It creates loyalty, not just compliance. Leaders who listen lead best. Empathy is strength in service.

→ **Where could empathy make you a stronger leader?**
Micro Challenge: Ask someone what support they need from you today.

Day 36: Boundaries Create Balance

Boundaries:
Life tips into overwhelm when everything is given equal access to your time. Boundaries restore balance by protecting space for rest and priorities. Saying no isn't selfish — it's survival. Balance grows when boundaries stand firm. Boundaries keep your life steady and your peace strong.

→ **Where could a boundary restore balance today?**
Micro Challenge: Block off one uninterrupted hour for yourself.

Day 37: Curiosity Fuels Discovery

Curiosity:
Discovery begins with curiosity. Asking new questions leads to new paths. Certainty keeps you where you are; curiosity moves you forward. Every breakthrough began with someone daring to wonder. Curiosity is the spark of progress. The more you ask, the more you uncover.

→ **What question could lead you forward today?**
Micro Challenge: Ask one "why" or "how" about something ordinary.

Day 38: Ordinary Into Treasure

Gratitude:
Ordinary days hold extraordinary moments if you notice them. Gratitude transforms routine into richness. The more you appreciate, the more you see. A grateful heart multiplies joy in even the smallest details. Gratitude makes life brighter without changing the circumstances. Treasure grows through thanks.

→ **What ordinary thing can you thank today?**
Micro Challenge: Write down three simple moments that made today better.

Day 39: Grit Stays When It's Boring

Grit:
When the buzz wears off, the middle can feel dull. Grit is showing up anyway. Progress is built in quiet, unglamorous reps no one sees. Enduring boredom is a strength most never train. Grit outlasts mood—and turns effort into growth.

→ **Where do you need grit to stay steady today?**
Micro Challenge: Do one extra rep, mile, or minute beyond quitting.

Day 40: Perspective Shrinks Fear

Perspective:
Fear magnifies problems until they feel impossible. Perspective reduces them to size. From a distance, most worries lose their power. Challenges that feel overwhelming today may look small tomorrow. Perspective helps courage rise. Fear fades when vision expands.

→ **How will this look in five years?**
Micro Challenge: Write one sentence reframing your fear as temporary.

Day 41: Growth Requires Effort

Growth:
Growth is never accidental. It's built through consistent effort. Skills expand when you practice. Confidence strengthens when you stretch. Progress is the fruit of showing up, not waiting. Effort creates growth that waiting never will.

→ **Where could effort grow you today?**
Micro Challenge: Spend 20 minutes practicing something you want to improve.

Day 42: Reflection Guides Change

Reflection:
Change without reflection risks repeating old mistakes. Reflection helps you see what to keep and what to release. It gives direction to growth and clarity to action. Looking back wisely makes moving forward smoother. Reflection is the compass of change.

→ **What change needs reflection first?**
Micro Challenge: Write down one thing to carry forward and one to leave behind.

Day 43: Focus Multiplies Momentum

Focus:
Momentum isn't built by doing everything — it's built by doing the right things repeatedly. Focus channels effort into progress. Distraction slows momentum until it stops. Protecting attention accelerates results. Focus is the accelerator of growth.

→ **Where could focus multiply momentum for you?**
Micro Challenge: Dedicate 30 distraction-free minutes to one key task.

Day 44: Courage Stands Alone

Category: Courage
Sometimes courage means standing alone. It's choosing values over popularity. Approval fades, but integrity remains. The bravest acts are often the loneliest. Courage builds strength when you refuse to bend. Standing alone today builds resilience tomorrow.

→ **Where might you need to stand alone?**
Micro Challenge: Say one truth even if no one agrees.

Day 45: Resilience Bends, Not Breaks

Resilience:
Rigidity breaks under pressure, but flexibility bends and survives. Resilience adapts without losing its core. The ability to adjust keeps you standing when conditions shift. Strength is proven in endurance, not in resistance to change. Resilience is survival in motion.

→ **Where could flexibility strengthen your resilience?**
Micro Challenge: Adapt one small plan instead of resisting it.

Day 46: Discipline Protects Integrity

Discipline:
Integrity is built in daily consistency. Discipline ensures your actions align with your values. Without it, words and behaviour drift apart. With it, you become reliable to yourself and others. Integrity is discipline practiced daily. Trust grows when discipline protects it.

→ **What action could reflect your integrity today?**
Micro Challenge: Keep one promise you've made, no matter how small.

Day 47: Energy Requires Rest

Energy:
Rest is not weakness — it's strength renewed. Energy drains with use, but rest restores it. Ignoring rest creates exhaustion that robs effectiveness. Choosing rest makes you sharper, calmer and more capable. Rest is fuel, not failure. Renewal powers endurance.

→ **Where do you need rest to regain energy?**
Micro Challenge: Take a 15-minute break today without screens.

Day 48: Relationships Need Repair

Relationships:
Conflict doesn't ruin relationships — lack of repair does. Every bond will face strain. Repairing with apology, care, or presence keeps them strong. Avoidance deepens cracks, but repair builds resilience. Strong relationships heal often. Repair is proof of love.

→ **Who could you repair with today?**
Micro Challenge: Reach out with one word of care or apology.

Day 49: Empathy Creates Safety

Empathy:
People open up when they feel safe. Empathy creates that safety by listening without judgment. Being understood strengthens trust. Empathy doesn't mean fixing; it means presence. Safety is the soil for growth. Empathy is the seed.

→ **Who needs safety through your empathy today?**
Micro Challenge: Listen fully without offering solutions.

Day 50: Boundaries Guard Energy

Boundaries:
Every yes costs energy. Boundaries protect your energy from being drained by everything. Saying no keeps you strong for what matters most. Without boundaries, exhaustion wins. With them, energy is guarded and renewed. Protect your fuel by protecting your limits.

→ **What boundary could protect your energy today?**
Micro Challenge: Decline one task that doesn't align with your priorities.

Day 51: Curiosity Makes Life Fresh

Curiosity:
Curiosity keeps life alive. Routine dulls the senses, but curiosity revives them. Seeing the world with fresh eyes makes even ordinary days interesting. Wonder transforms boredom into discovery. Curiosity makes every day new.

→ **What could curiosity refresh for you today?**
Micro Challenge: Try one new thing you haven't done before.

Day 52: Gratitude Reframes the Day

Gratitude:
Every day carries stress, but gratitude reframes it. Counting what's steady helps balance what's shaky. Gratitude doesn't erase pressure, but it shifts perspective. Focusing on blessings makes burdens lighter. Gratitude rewrites the day.

→ **What bright spot could you name today?**
Micro Challenge: Write down three positives before going to sleep.

Day 53: Grit Beats Excuses

Grit:
Excuses are easy; grit is hard. Excuses stall progress, but grit keeps moving anyway. Success belongs to those who act despite reasons to stop. Grit is the decision to continue when it's inconvenient. Outlasting excuses is strength in motion.

→ **What excuse do you need to silence today?**
Micro Challenge: Take one step on something you've been delaying.

Day 54: Perspective Brings Calm

Perspective:
Stress magnifies when you see only the problem. Perspective widens the lens and restores calm. Most challenges are smaller when seen alongside the whole picture. Balance comes from a bigger view. Perspective creates peace by changing focus.

→ **How could a wider view bring calm today?**
Micro Challenge: Write down three things going right despite stress.

Day 55: Growth Loves Discomfort

Growth:
Discomfort isn't failure — it's growth in progress. Stretching into the unknown feels awkward but builds capacity. Avoiding discomfort avoids progress. Each uncomfortable step is a sign of expansion. Growth always travels with discomfort.

→ **Where could discomfort mean growth today?**
Micro Challenge: Take one action that feels slightly uncomfortable.

Day 56: Reflection Strengthens Learning

Reflection:
Learning deepens when you pause to reflect. Without it, lessons slip away. Reflection strengthens memory and meaning. Looking back turns information into wisdom. Every reflection adds to your growth. Reflection is learning reinforced.

→ **What lesson needs reflection today?**
Micro Challenge: Write three lines about what you learned this week.

Day 57: Focus Protects Time

Focus:
Time is wasted when scattered. Focus protects it by directing effort to essentials. When you focus, hours stretch and productivity rises. Without focus, time leaks into distractions. Protect your hours with sharp attention. Focus saves your time.

→ **What deserves your time most today?**
Micro Challenge: Block one hour for your top task, distraction-free.

Day 58: Courage Means Honesty

Courage:
Honesty requires courage. Speaking truth risks discomfort, but it builds trust. Without honesty, relationships weaken. Courage says what needs to be said with care. Bravery often sounds like honesty. Truth strengthens every connection.

→ **Where could honesty show courage today?**
Micro Challenge: Speak one truth kindly but clearly.

Day 59: Resilience Finds Hope

Resilience:
Resilience isn't ignoring pain — it's holding hope through it. Hope provides strength to endure and to rebuild. Even in hardship, resilience whispers, "This isn't the end." With hope, resilience rises again and again. Hope is the anchor of endurance.

→ **What hope could strengthen you today?**
Micro Challenge: Write down one reason tomorrow could be better.

February Workbook – Consistency Tracker

Consistency is what turns effort into results. This month was about building steady rhythms and showing up even on the hard days. Use this page to reflect on your patterns, both strong and weak and set a course for steadiness going forward.

1. Reflection

Where did I stay consistent this month?

_____
_____
_____

Where did I break my streaks and why?

_____
_____
_____

What habits are becoming automatic for me?

_____
_____
_____

What excuses kept showing up?

_____
_____
_____

What routine will I carry into March?

_____
_____
_____

2. Journaling Prompt

Think of a moment this month where you almost quit but didn't. Write about what you felt in that moment and what you gained by staying in it.

_____
_____
_____

3. Exercise

Create a consistency chain. For each day this month, mark an X if you showed up. Circle any missed days and write why. Look for patterns.

[Use the space below to draw, sketch, or note your ideas.]

_____
_____
_____

March — Renewal

March carries the first signs of spring. The days stretch longer, the light grows brighter and the air itself seems to whisper begin again. Renewal is the theme of this month—not the reckless tossing aside of what came before, but the gentle invitation to breathe new life into the habits, hopes and goals that matter most. Renewal doesn't mean erasing what you've done; it means recognising what's worth continuing and giving it the energy it deserves.

By now, you've planted seeds in January and practiced steadiness through February. March is about refreshing that commitment. Renewal doesn't demand starting over from scratch; it asks for recommitment with clarity. Maybe some routines have faltered. That's fine. Renewal says, *pick them back up*. Maybe you've noticed certain practices bearing fruit. Renewal says, *nurture them*. Growth is not a straight line; it's a cycle of returning, refreshing and refining. This month is your chance to revisit your foundations and decide where to lean in a little more.

Curiosity belongs here too. Renewal thrives when you ask fresh questions: What's working? What feels stale? What could I approach with new energy? The more curious you are, the more opportunities you'll find for subtle but powerful shifts. Curiosity stops growth from becoming rigid; it keeps the process alive. March gives permission to experiment, to explore and to rediscover joy in the very act of trying.

And joy matters deeply this month. Renewal doesn't have to feel heavy or forced. It can be light, playful and energising. Think of laughter, sunlight and the way a sprout pushes through soil with quiet determination. That is renewal at work—resilient, hopeful and persistent. When you let joy into your daily practice, renewal becomes less about discipline and more about delight.

March invites you to live like spring. Clear away the clutter of what no longer serves. Refresh the habits that still matter. Plant again where growth has stalled. Each step you take this month is a declaration that new beginnings are always possible, no matter the season.

This is your reminder: renewal is never out of reach. You can begin again, right here, right now—with energy, with intention and with hope.

Day 60: Discipline Shapes Identity

Discipline:
Your identity is formed by what you repeat. Discipline makes your habits consistent with who you want to be. Every disciplined choice shapes character. Without it, you drift from your values. With it, you build self-trust and strength. Discipline is identity in action.

→ **What habit shapes your identity today?**
Micro Challenge: Do one action that reflects your best self.

Day 61: Energy Flows from Purpose

Energy:
Exhaustion often comes from meaningless effort. Purpose fuels energy beyond rest or caffeine. When you know why it matters, strength multiplies. Purpose connects struggle to meaning. Energy flows when the reason is clear. Purpose is power.

→ **What purpose fuels you today?**
Micro Challenge: Write one sentence starting with "I'm doing this because…"

Day 62: Relationships Require Effort

Relationships:
Relationships don't stay strong by accident — they require effort. Small acts of care, attention and kindness keep them alive. Neglect weakens, but effort restores. People thrive when they feel valued daily. Relationships are gardens you must tend.

→ **Who could use your effort today?**
Micro Challenge: Send one message of encouragement.

Day 63: Empathy Softens Conflict

Empathy:
Conflict hardens when no one feels understood. Empathy softens it by listening with compassion. It doesn't erase differences but makes space for resolution. Empathy shifts battles into conversations. People soften when they feel seen.

→ **Where could empathy ease conflict today?**
Micro Challenge: Repeat back what you heard before sharing your view.

Day 64: Boundaries Protect Your Future

Boundaries:
Every commitment today shapes tomorrow. Boundaries protect your future from being consumed by present noise. Saying no now makes room for long-term yes. Without boundaries, tomorrow gets sacrificed. Guard your future by guarding today.

→ **What boundary could protect your tomorrow?**
Micro Challenge: Decline one thing that doesn't serve your future self.
Top of Form

Day 65: Curiosity Sparks Possibility

Curiosity:
Certainty keeps you in place, but curiosity opens doors. Every new idea, solution, or discovery begins with a question. Curiosity asks what else could be true, what else could work, what else might exist. It pushes against limits and finds fresh ground. The more you ask, the more life expands. Possibility grows where curiosity is alive.

→ **What question could create possibility today?**
Micro Challenge: Ask one new "what if" about your current challenge.

Day 66: Gratitude Balances Pressure

Gratitude:
Pressure narrows your vision until you see only stress. Gratitude widens it again by noticing what's steady and good. Even in chaos, something remains worth appreciating. Gratitude doesn't erase pressure, but it makes it lighter. Balance comes from what you count. The more you notice, the more you endure.

→ **What can you be grateful for in this moment?**
Micro Challenge: Write three things keeping you steady right now.

Day 67: Grit Pushes Through Silence

Grit:
Progress isn't always visible. Sometimes grit means showing up when no one claps or notices. Quiet persistence builds strength and momentum unseen. Over time, these hidden efforts produce real breakthroughs. Grit is consistency without applause. Strength grows in silence.

→ **Where could grit keep you steady today?**
Micro Challenge: Do one action without telling anyone — let the work speak.

Day 68: Perspective Restores Calm

Perspective:
Stress grows when a problem takes over your whole view. Perspective reminds you it's only part of the story. Stepping back shows what's still working, what's still steady, what's still good. The challenge shrinks in proportion to the bigger picture. Calm returns with a wider lens. Perspective creates peace.

→ **What else is true besides your problem?**
Micro Challenge: Write three good things happening alongside your stress.

Day 69: Growth Loves Challenge

Growth:
Challenge is the training ground for growth. Without resistance, skills stagnate. Every struggle stretches your capacity and prepares you for more. Growth rarely feels easy — it feels uncomfortable, awkward, sometimes discouraging. But those feelings are proof that expansion is happening. Challenge is growth in disguise.

→ **What challenge could grow you today?**
Micro Challenge: Take on one task slightly harder than your comfort zone.

Day 70: Reflection Creates Self-Awareness

Reflection:
Without reflection, blind spots remain blind. Pausing to review choices helps you see where you're aligned and where you're drifting. Self-awareness grows from reflection, not from constant motion. Awareness is power — it turns mistakes into teachers. Reflection transforms experience into wisdom. Look back to move forward well.

→ **What moment deserves reflection today?**
Micro Challenge: Write down one lesson from this week and how you'll use it.

Day 71: Focus Protects Energy

Focus:
Energy leaks through scattered attention. Focus keeps it contained and powerful. What you direct your mind toward grows stronger. Distraction multiplies exhaustion, but focus multiplies results. Protecting focus protects energy. A single priority done well outshines ten done halfway.

→ **Where should your energy be directed today?**
Micro Challenge: Set a 25-minute timer and work without distraction.

Day 72: Courage Faces the Mirror

Courage:
The hardest truth to face is your own. Courage looks in the mirror and admits flaws honestly. Denial delays growth, but honesty accelerates it. Facing yourself isn't weakness — it's the first step toward strength. Courage with yourself creates freedom. Bravery begins with truth.

→ **What truth about yourself are you avoiding?**
Micro Challenge: Write down one habit you need to change and one step to start.

Day 73: Resilience is Flexibility

Resilience:
Rigid strength breaks under pressure, but resilience bends. Flexibility allows you to keep moving when plans shift. The goal can remain the same, but the path can change. Adaptation isn't weakness; it's survival. Resilience grows every time you pivot without giving up. Bend and endure.

→ **Where do you need more flexibility today?**
Micro Challenge: Adjust one plan instead of abandoning it.

Day 74: Discipline Shapes Character

Discipline:
Character isn't proven in big moments but in daily choices. Discipline ensures those choices match your values. Each consistent action builds integrity. Without discipline, intentions drift; with it, words and actions align. Over time, small habits shape who you are. Discipline writes your character.

→ **What daily act reflects your character today?**
Micro Challenge: Do one habit that aligns with your values.

Day 75: Energy Grows from Movement

Energy:
Energy doesn't just come from rest — it also comes from motion. Moving your body sparks momentum. Physical action wakes mental energy. Waiting until you feel energised rarely works. Sometimes the act of moving creates the energy itself. Movement is fuel.

→ **What movement could energise you today?**
Micro Challenge: Take a brisk 10-minute walk or stretch break.

Day 76: Relationships Are Built in Listening

Relationships:
People want to feel heard more than persuaded. Listening is one of the strongest ways to show care. Interruptions break trust, but listening builds it. Presence in listening is love in action. When you listen deeply, you connect deeply. Trust grows in silence.

→ **Who needs your full listening today?**
Micro Challenge: Ask one question and listen without interrupting.

Day 77: Empathy Heals Division

Empathy:
Division grows when assumptions multiply. Empathy interrupts it by choosing to understand first. Listening with compassion creates bridges. You don't need to agree to care. Empathy transforms distance into connection. Healing begins when you choose to see another's side.

→ **Where could empathy heal division today?**
Micro Challenge: Ask someone what they see that you don't.

Day 78: Boundaries Guard Mental Space

Boundaries:
Mental clutter comes from allowing everything in. Boundaries protect your inner space by deciding what thoughts and inputs belong. Without them, your peace is invaded. With them, calm and clarity remain. Protecting your mind is as important as protecting your time. Boundaries defend your mental health.

→ **What thought or input could you block today?**
Micro Challenge: Limit one source of negativity for the day.

Day 79: Curiosity Fuels Learning

Curiosity:
Learning doesn't stop with school — it grows with curiosity. Asking why and how keeps your mind active. Curiosity drives innovation and keeps life interesting. Without it, you stagnate; with it, you expand. Every question opens a door. Curiosity feeds growth.

→ **What could you learn today through curiosity?**
Micro Challenge: Ask one question that stretches your knowledge.

Day 80: Gratitude Strengthens Relationships

Gratitude:
Unspoken appreciation weakens bonds over time. Expressed gratitude strengthens them. People thrive when they feel noticed and valued. Saying thank you consistently builds connection. Gratitude is the glue of relationships. Appreciation keeps bonds alive.

→ **Who deserves your thanks today?**
Micro Challenge: Tell one person specifically why you appreciate them.

Day 81: Grit Outlasts Doubt

Grit:
Doubt tempts you to stop, but grit outlasts it. Perseverance weakens doubt's grip. Each time you continue despite uncertainty, you grow stronger. Progress belongs to those who endure longer. Grit is doubt's undoing. Keep going and prove it wrong.

→ **Where do you need grit today?**
Micro Challenge: Take one step on a goal you're unsure about.

Day 82: Perspective Brings Balance

Perspective:
Problems seem bigger when they take up your whole view. Perspective reminds you they're just part of your story. A balanced lens shows what's good alongside what's hard. Seeing both brings calm and strength. Perspective restores balance.

→ **What good stands beside your challenge today?**
Micro Challenge: Write three steady things in your life right now.

Day 83: Growth Needs Courage

Growth:
Every step of growth requires courage. You must risk failure, discomfort, or rejection to expand. Courage moves you into spaces you haven't mastered yet. Without it, growth stalls. Each brave act is growth in motion. Courage and growth are inseparable.

→ **What risk could grow you today?**
Micro Challenge: Take one action you've avoided out of fear.

Day 84: Reflection Creates Meaning

Reflection:
Life without reflection feels like noise without melody. Reflection gives meaning to experiences by helping you connect dots. It transforms chaos into clarity. Pausing to reflect reveals lessons and progress. Reflection doesn't change events, but it changes how you understand them. Meaning grows in the pause.

→ **What moment could hold meaning today?**
Micro Challenge. Spend five minutes journaling about one recent experience.

Day 85: Focus Sharpens Strength

Focus:
Strength grows when it's concentrated. Spreading yourself thin dilutes progress. Focus directs effort toward mastery. What you repeat with attention becomes what you excel at. Mediocrity comes from scatter; excellence comes from focus. Strength sharpens where attention stays.

→ **Where could focus make you stronger today?**
Micro Challenge: Spend 30 minutes improving one skill deliberately.

Day 86: Courage Confronts Fear

Courage:
Fear grows when avoided but shrinks when faced. Courage doesn't mean fear vanishes — it means you move anyway. Each confrontation reduces fear's hold. Confidence comes through repeated acts of bravery. Courage frees you to live more fully. Face the fear and it weakens.

→ **What fear could you face today?**
Micro Challenge: Take one small step into something you've delayed.

Day 87: Resilience Restarts Again

Resilience:
Resilience is the strength to restart, no matter how many times you've stopped. Each restart proves failure isn't final. The willingness to begin again builds grit and humility. Progress isn't lost when you restart — it's built. Resilience is restarted in motion.

→ **Where do you need to begin again?**
Micro Challenge: Restart one dropped habit or goal today.

Day 88: Discipline Builds Confidence

Discipline:
Confidence grows from proof, not pep talks. Discipline provides that proof by showing you can rely on yourself. Each kept promise builds belief. Skipped commitments erode trust, but discipline restores it. Confidence follows discipline like shadow follows light. Trust yourself through action.

→ **What discipline could build your confidence today?**
Micro Challenge: Keep one small promise before the day ends.

Day 89: Energy Flows from Connection

Energy:
Some people drain you, others energise you. Connection with uplifting people renews your energy. A good conversation can recharge more than rest. Choose connections that strengthen your spirit. Energy grows in safe, supportive relationships. Who you connect with matters.

→ **Who lifts your energy when you connect?**
Micro Challenge: Reach out to one energising person today.

Day 90: Relationships Need Honesty

Relationships:
Honesty keeps relationships alive. Without it, connections weaken under pretence. Truth, spoken with care, builds trust. Even hard honesty strengthens bonds when given respectfully. Real relationships require real words. Honesty is love in practice.

→ **Who needs honesty from you today?**
Micro Challenge: Speak one truth with kindness.

March Workbook – Fresh Start

March signals renewal. Just as the season begins to turn, this is a chance to restart what stalled and breathe fresh life into your habits and mindset. Use this page to let go of what's dragging you down and commit to what lifts you up.

1. Reflection

What areas of my life feel renewed this month?

_____
_____
_____

What habits need a clean restart?

_____
_____
_____

What am I ready to leave behind for good?

_____
_____
_____

What brought me the most energy?

_____
_____
_____

What new direction excites me?

_____

_____

_____

2. Journaling Prompt
Journal freely on this: 'If I gave myself full permission to start again, I would…' Let your pen move without editing yourself.

_____

_____

_____

3. Exercise
Create two columns: 'Old Patterns to Release' and 'Fresh Habits to Begin'. Fill at least three in each. Circle one to commit to in April.

[Use the space below to draw, sketch, or note your ideas.]

_____

_____

_____

April — Momentum

April is the month when effort starts to echo. Momentum is a powerful force. By now, you've built habits, endured resistance and learned to renew your focus. You begin to feel the weight of compounding effort. What was once difficult starts to feel natural. What was once forced begins to flow. That's not luck; it's the quiet interest earned on every small deposit of consistency.

Momentum doesn't make everything effortless—it makes forward motion easier to choose. Your past choices are now carrying you. Each day you showed up in January, each act of steadiness in February and each recommitment in March has built a current. April invites you to lean into that current and let it do some of the lifting. Ease is not a warning sign; it's a sign the system is working.

Guard your focus. Momentum is fragile when distractions creep in. This month, you may feel strong enough to juggle everything—don't. Momentum thrives on direction. Choose the few things that matter most and give them your full energy. A narrow channel makes the river stronger. Protect the first hour of your day, batch similar tasks and single task the work that moves the needle. Say no more often so your yes can travel farther.

Courage belongs here too. Momentum is the best time to stretch into something bigger because your base is solid. Push a little further: add five minutes to the session, lift the slightly heavier weight, hold the last repeat with composure, send the email you've been avoiding. Attempt what once felt out of reach and trust your habits to carry the load. April rewards boldness that is grounded, not reckless.

Treat momentum like a snowball rolling downhill: each turn gathers mass and speed. Don't stop it unnecessarily. Protect it with simple rules—start before you scroll, finish what you open, leave a clear next action for tomorrow. Guide it with weekly check-ins: What worked? What dragged? What small tweak would make next week smoother? Remember, rest does not break momentum, unintentional drift does. Plan recovery on purpose and you'll roll farther.

April is the month where progress feels real—where you catch yourself doing hard things calmly. Lean in. Keep the channel narrow, the steps deliberate and the courage steady. Trust the process you've built. Let momentum carry you—and then add one deliberate push of your own.

Day 91: Empathy Creates Connection

Empathy:
Connection deepens when empathy is present. Empathy says, "I see you, I hear you." People don't need fixing — they need presence. Listening with care strengthens bonds more than advice. Empathy turns distance into closeness. Connection thrives when empathy leads.

→ **Who could you connect with through empathy today?**
Micro Challenge: Ask someone how they're really doing and listen fully.

Day 92: Boundaries Protect Peace

Boundaries:
Without boundaries, chaos creeps into your peace. Limits protect the calm you need. Boundaries aren't selfish; they're necessary. They create space for rest, clarity and joy. Protecting peace means protecting yourself. Boundaries are shields of sanity.

→ **What boundary could protect your peace today?**
Micro Challenge: Block one hour for yourself with no interruptions.

Day 93: Curiosity Opens Creativity

Curiosity:
Creativity often begins with curiosity. Asking fresh questions opens new ideas. Assumptions recycle the old, but curiosity discovers the new. Every creative leap begins with a curious thought. Wonder makes imagination possible. Curiosity lights the spark.

→ **What question could spark creativity today?**
Micro Challenge: Ask "what if" about one routine task.

Day 94: Gratitude Expands Joy

Gratitude:
Joy expands when gratitude is practiced daily. Gratitude turns scarcity into abundance. It doesn't ignore struggle but balances it with appreciation. The more you count blessings, the richer life feels. Joy multiplies where gratitude grows.

→ **What joy could gratitude expand today?**
Micro Challenge: Write three things you're grateful for before bed.

Day 95: Grit Finishes Strong

Grit:
Starting is easy; finishing requires grit. Endings test endurance more than beginnings. Grit keeps you steady when motivation fades. Finishing builds strength and confidence for future challenges. Grit makes completion possible. Strong finishes build strong belief.

→ **Where do you need grit to finish strong?**
Micro Challenge: Complete one task you've been avoiding.

Day 96: Perspective Restores Hope

Perspective:
Hopelessness grows when problems dominate your vision. Perspective restores hope by reminding you of the bigger story. Most struggles are temporary, not permanent. A wider view shows that better days remain possible. Hope lives where perspective expands.

→ **What hope could perspective restore today?**
Micro Challenge: Write one reason this situation will pass.

Day 97: Growth is Practice, Not Perfection

Growth:
Perfection stops progress before it starts. Growth doesn't require flawless execution, only steady practice. Each imperfect attempt builds skill and confidence. Over time, progress compounds, even when it feels messy. Growth is born from showing up, not from being perfect. Practice creates expansion.

→ **Where could practice matter more than perfection today?**
Micro Challenge: Do one small action imperfectly but consistently.

Day 98: Reflection Reveals Patterns

Reflection:
Life leaves clues, but only if you pause to notice them. Reflection helps you see patterns of success and failure. Without it, mistakes repeat and progress hides. Reflection turns hindsight into insight. Patterns give direction for the future. Wisdom is found in review.

→ **What pattern is reflection showing you?**
Micro Challenge: Write down one repeated theme in your week.

Day 99: Focus Creates Impact

Focus:
Impact doesn't come from spreading thin — it comes from depth. Focus takes scattered effort and channels it into meaningful results. When you try to do everything, nothing gets done well. Choosing one priority creates momentum that multiplies. Focus is the path to significance. Impact follows attention.

→ **Where should your focus be today?**
Micro Challenge: Pick your top task and complete it before touching the rest.

Day 100: Courage Takes the First Step

Courage:
The first step often feels like the heaviest. Courage lightens it by moving anyway. Waiting for fear to disappear only delays progress. Bravery grows stronger in motion. The act of starting is often scarier than the task itself. Courage begins where hesitation ends.

→ **What first step could courage create for you today?**
Micro Challenge: Take one step forward, no matter how small.

Day 101: Resilience Finds a Way

Resilience:
Resilience doesn't deny obstacles — it works around them. When one path blocks, resilience looks for another. It's the ability to adjust without giving up. Challenges don't end the journey; they redirect it. Resilience turns walls into detours, not dead ends. Adaptation is its strength.

→ **Where do you need to find another way?**
Micro Challenge: Try one alternate approach to your current problem.

Day 102: Discipline Strengthens Identity

Discipline:
Who you become is shaped by what you consistently do. Discipline aligns your actions with your values. Without it, identity drifts; with it, character solidifies. Each small, disciplined act is evidence of who you are. Identity is built daily, not declared once. Discipline writes the story of you.

→ **What habit reflects your identity today?**
Micro Challenge: Do one action that matches who you want to be.

Day 103: Energy Comes from Purpose

Energy:
Tiredness isn't always physical — sometimes it's a lack of meaning. Purpose fuels energy when nothing else works. When you know why you're doing something, strength rises. Tasks tied to purpose feel lighter, even when hard. Energy flows where purpose lives. Meaning creates momentum.

→ **What purpose could energise you today?**
Micro Challenge: Write one sentence: "I'm doing this because…"

Day 104: Relationships Need Repair

Relationships:
Every relationship faces strain, but repair keeps it alive. Avoidance deepens the crack, while honesty heals it. Repair requires humility, apology and care. It doesn't erase conflict but transforms it into connection. Strong bonds aren't conflict-free; they're resilient through repair.

→ **Who could you repair with today?**
Micro Challenge: Send one message to begin rebuilding a strained relationship.

Day 105: Empathy Creates Understanding

Empathy:
Assumptions create distance; empathy closes it. To understand someone's world, you must listen with openness. Empathy doesn't erase differences but makes space for respect. Connection grows when people feel seen. Empathy builds bridges over judgment. Understanding is its gift.

→ **Who needs understanding from you today?**
Micro Challenge: Ask one person about their perspective before sharing yours.

Day 106: Boundaries Guard Your Time

Boundaries:
Time is your most valuable resource. Without boundaries, it slips into other people's agendas. Boundaries protect your priorities from being consumed. Saying no creates room for what matters most. Guarding your hours is guarding your life. Boundaries are time's defence.

→ **What boundary could protect your time today?**
Micro Challenge: Block off one hour for a personal priority.

Day 107: Curiosity Creates Joy

Curiosity:
Curiosity isn't only for solving problems — it makes life brighter. Looking at the ordinary with wonder adds delight to daily moments. Asking, "What's here I've missed?" renews joy. Curiosity makes the familiar feel fresh. Joy grows with discovery. Wonder is a choice.

→ **Where could curiosity spark joy today?**
Micro Challenge: Try one small new experience before the day ends.

Day 108: Gratitude Expands Enough

Gratitude:
Scarcity whispers, "Not enough." Gratitude replies, "Plenty." By noticing what you already have, you change the story. Gratitude makes life feel fuller without adding anything new. Enough is a perspective, not a possession. Gratitude expands your sense of abundance.

→ **What do you already have enough of?**
Micro Challenge: Write three areas where your needs are already met.

Day 109: Grit Outlasts Excuses

Grit:
Excuses multiply when effort feels heavy. Grit silences them with action. The difference between quitting and succeeding is often one more attempt. Grit is doing what matters even when reasons to stop appear. Excuses fade when persistence holds. Endurance wins.

→ **Where do you need grit today?**
Micro Challenge: Do one task you've been postponing with no delay.

Day 110: Perspective Restores Hope

Perspective:
Problems feel permanent when seen up close. Perspective pulls you back to see they're temporary chapters. Most struggles pass sooner than you expect. Hope grows when perspective widens. Looking beyond today restores faith in tomorrow. Vision lifts discouragement.

→ **What wider view could restore hope today?**
Micro Challenge: Write one reason this situation will pass.

Day 111: Growth Demands Change

Growth:
You cannot grow while staying the same. Change stretches your capacity and identity. It may feel risky, but it's the soil where growth happens. Every small shift expands what's possible. Growth is change in motion. Safety keeps you still; change moves you forward.

→ **What change could fuel your growth today?**
Micro Challenge: Start one new habit or drop one old one.

Day 112: Reflection Builds Wisdom

Reflection:
Experience doesn't automatically make you wiser — reflection does. Without reflection, lessons slip away. Pausing helps you see what worked and what didn't. Wisdom is learning applied, not just lived. Reflection transforms mistakes into teachers and victories into guides. Wisdom is reflection in action.

→ **What lesson needs reflection today?**
Micro Challenge: Write down one insight and how you'll apply it.

Day 113: Focus Creates Simplicity

Focus:
Life feels overwhelming when everything matters equally. Focus cuts through clutter and highlights what's essential. Doing less with depth beats doing more with distraction. Simplicity comes from attention, not chance. The clearer your focus, the lighter your load. Focus simplifies life.

→ **What one focus would simplify your day?**
Micro Challenge: Complete your most important task before noon.

Day 114: Courage Chooses Vulnerability

Courage:
Vulnerability feels risky but builds connection. Admitting weakness, asking for help, or sharing feelings requires bravery. Courage isn't always loud — sometimes it's quiet honesty. Vulnerability clears walls and invites trust. The strongest bonds are formed in truth. Courage chooses openness.

→ **Where could vulnerability serve you today?**
Micro Challenge: Share one truth you usually keep guarded.

Day 115: Resilience Holds Steady

Resilience:
Resilience doesn't always mean moving fast — sometimes it means holding steady. Staying calm in uncertainty is its own strength. Endurance is often about presence, not speed. Resilience keeps you grounded until clarity returns. Steadiness is survival.

→ **Where could you hold steady today?**
Micro Challenge: Take three deep breaths before reacting to stress.

Day 116: Discipline Builds Legacy

Discipline:
Legacy isn't built in a single moment but in repeated habits. What you do daily becomes the story you leave behind. Discipline ensures that story is consistent and clear. Without it, legacies fade; with it, they endure. Each disciplined act is a brick in the structure of your life. Discipline builds legacy.

→ **What daily habit could shape your legacy?**
Micro Challenge: Do one action that reflects the person you want to be remembered as.

Day 117: Energy Needs Boundaries

Energy:
Energy leaks when you say yes to everything. Boundaries keep your strength from scattering. Protecting your energy isn't selfish — it's essential. Guarding your fuel helps you show up fully where it matters. Without boundaries, burnout takes over. Energy needs defence.

→ **Where could a boundary protect your energy today?**
Micro Challenge: Say no to one draining demand.

Day 118: Relationships Grow with Appreciation

Relationships:
Appreciation fuels connection. Without it, relationships weaken; with it, they thrive. People want to feel noticed and valued. Small acknowledgments of care build lasting trust. Gratitude spoken keeps bonds alive. Appreciation is the glue of connection.

→ **Who deserves appreciation from you today?**
Micro Challenge: Express thanks to one person before the day ends.

Day 119: Empathy Softens Judgment

Empathy:
Judgment closes hearts; empathy opens them. When you pause to consider what someone might be carrying, perspective shifts. Empathy doesn't excuse harm but humanises the person. It makes room for compassion over condemnation. Connection grows where empathy leads.

→ **Who could you see with more empathy today?**
Micro Challenge: Imagine three pressures that person may be facing before you respond.

Day 120: Boundaries Strengthen Trust

Boundaries:
Boundaries don't push people away — they teach respect. Clear limits show others how to treat you. Without boundaries, resentment grows; with them, trust deepens. Respect is built on clarity, not on over giving. Boundaries strengthen both relationships and self-respect.

→ **What boundary could strengthen trust today?**
Micro Challenge: State one limit calmly and confidently.

April Workbook – Momentum Builder

Momentum is built from small, repeated actions that gather strength over time. This month was about recognising where your momentum grows and how to keep it rolling when obstacles appear.

1. Reflection

Where did momentum pick up this month?

_____
_____
_____

Where did it stall and why?

_____
_____
_____

What helped me feel unstoppable?

_____
_____
_____

What slowed me down?

_____
_____
_____

What do I need to double down on next month?

_____
_____
_____

22. Journaling Prompt
Write about a time when small steps suddenly added up to something bigger. How did that feel? What did it teach you?

_____
_____
_____

3. Exercise
Draw a snowball rolling downhill. Inside the snowball, list habits that build momentum. Around it, write distractions that slow you. Add arrows showing which pushes you forward and which pull you back.

[Use the space below to draw, sketch, or note your ideas.]

_____
_____
_____

May — Endurance

May is the month after the spark—the stretch of road where the scenery repeats and the rhythm matters more than the view. By now, the shine of new beginnings has worn away. The work feels familiar, maybe even repetitive. This is where progress slows and endurance takes over. Growth isn't always exciting and that's why grit is essential. Grit is choosing to keep showing up when no one is watching, when the metrics stall, when the novelty has faded and the only thing left is you and the next small step.

Endurance is staying when motivation dips. It's believing that quiet effort compounds, even when you can't yet see the curve of improvement. May teaches you to love the grind—not because it's glamorous, but because it forges strength in ways shortcuts never can. Steady weeks change you more than dramatic days.

This month asks you to stretch—one step beyond comfort, one rep past easy, one page past done. The urge to stop will arrive right at the border of progress. Notice it. Breathe. Take the next measured step. That's the proof you're after: not perfection, but evidence. Each time you push through the soft ceiling, you collect a receipt for your own resilience. Proof becomes confidence; confidence becomes fuel.

To carry this pace, protect your systems. Keep start times consistent. Prep the night before. Use simple checklists. Track effort, not just outcomes: minutes moved, sessions completed, promises kept. When boredom hums, reduce the friction—shorten the warm-up barrier, lay out your kit, make the first action obvious.

Celebrate micro-wins, then move on without fanfare. Momentum loves tidy finishes.

Gratitude is endurance's quiet partner. Without gratitude, the grind sours. With it, you recognise the gift of capacity: lungs that work, legs that hold, a mind that returns to the task. Be grateful for the ordinary day that lets you practice. Gratitude lightens discipline; it keeps effort from hardening into resentment.

Plan recovery on purpose. Endurance is not an unbroken line; it's effort balanced with repair. Sleep, fuel, walk, breathe, stretch. Rest is part of the work—the thing that lets you come back tomorrow with steadier hands.

May is about persistence. You won't always see immediate results, but every honest repetition matters. Endurance is the silent work that makes future breakthroughs possible. Trust the lane you're in. Keep the cadence. Do today's piece. Then do tomorrow's. Progress is often quiet right before it becomes obvious

Day 121: Curiosity Fuels Growth

Curiosity:
Growth begins with the courage to ask questions. Curiosity expands your world beyond assumptions. It sparks innovation, learning and connection. Each new question is a step toward discovery. Without curiosity, you repeat; with it, you evolve. Growth thrives on curiosity.

→ **What question could grow you today?**
Micro Challenge: Ask one person about something they know that you don't.

Day 122: Gratitude Grounds You

Gratitude:
When life feels chaotic, gratitude steadies you. It anchors attention to what's still good. Gratitude shifts the nervous system from stress to calm. It reminds you not everything is chaos. Even small thanks bring grounding. Gratitude is balance in motion.

→ **What grounds you today?**
Micro Challenge: Write down three things holding you steady.

Day 123: Grit Chooses Consistency

Grit:
Talent shines briefly, but grit endures. Grit is the choice to show up consistently, especially when progress is invisible. Each repeated effort compounds into strength. Consistency outlasts talent, luck and mood. Grit wins by refusing to stop. Consistency is grit's gift.

→ **Where do you need consistency most today?**
Micro Challenge: Do one small action for the same goal as yesterday.

Day 124: Perspective Shrinks Problems

Perspective:
Problems feel massive when you stare only at them. Perspective reminds you they're only part of the picture. From distance, most problems shrink in scale. The challenge may still be real, but it's no longer everything. Perspective makes problems manageable.

→ **What else could you notice alongside the problem?**
Micro Challenge: Write down three good things that remain true.

Day 125: Growth Requires Effort

Growth:
Growth isn't given — it's earned. Each step takes effort and persistence. Comfort feels easier but produces little change. Struggle stretches you into strength. Growth always costs something, but it pays more back. The effort is worth it.

→ **Where could effort fuel your growth today?**
Micro Challenge: Spend 15 minutes on one growth habit.

Day 126: Reflection Shows Progress

Reflection:
Progress often hides in the daily grind. Reflection reveals it by showing how far you've come. Looking back proves consistency works. Without reflection, you underestimate growth. With it, you encourage yourself to keep going. Reflection is progress revealed.

→ **Where have you grown that you haven't noticed?**
Micro Challenge: List three ways you've improved in the last 3 months.

Day 127: Focus Directs Power

Focus:
Energy without focus scatters like light through clouds. Focus directs it into power, like a laser. Choosing one priority channels effort into impact. Without focus, activity multiplies but results vanish. With focus, power is magnified. Direction creates strength.

→ **What priority deserves your full power today?**
Micro Challenge: Spend 30 minutes on your highest-value task.

Day 128: Courage Builds Connection

Courage:
Relationships deepen when you risk honesty. Sharing your real thoughts or feelings requires bravery. Vulnerability invites closeness others can't create alone. Courage in connection strengthens bonds. Openness is the door to intimacy. Bravery builds closeness.

→ **Who could you open up to today?**
Micro Challenge: Share one genuine thought you've been holding back.

Day 129: Resilience Holds Hope

Resilience:
Resilience is not about ignoring hardship — it's about holding hope through it. Hope fuels endurance when strength feels low. It reminds you that struggle is temporary and that better days are ahead. Even in dark seasons, resilience whispers, "This is not the end." Hope is resilience's quiet ally. With it, you rise again and again.

→ **What hope could strengthen you today?**
Micro Challenge. Write down one reason tomorrow could be brighter.

Day 130: Discipline Creates Confidence

Discipline:
Confidence isn't built by words but by evidence. Each disciplined act is proof you can rely on yourself. When you keep promises, trust in yourself grows. Skipping discipline erodes belief, but staying consistent strengthens it. Confidence follows discipline like shadow follows light. Self-trust is earned daily.

→ **What action could build confidence today?**
Micro Challenge: Keep one small promise before the day ends.

Day 131: Energy Flows Through Renewal

Energy:
Energy doesn't come from constant work — it comes from balance. Rest, play and renewal restore what effort drains. Ignoring renewal leads to collapse, while honouring it builds longevity. Energy is sustained by cycles, not by force. Choosing renewal is choosing strength. Restoration is fuel for tomorrow.

→ **Where do you need renewal today?**
Micro Challenge: Take 15 minutes for something that restores you.

Day 132: Relationships Need Effort

Relationships:
Strong relationships are built on effort, not accident. Daily acts of care keep bonds alive. Neglect weakens them, but intentional effort strengthens them. A quick word of kindness or a moment of presence can make a difference. Love grows where effort is shown. Relationships thrive when nurtured.

→ **Who needs your effort today?**
Micro Challenge: Send one encouraging message to someone you value.

Day 133: Empathy Builds Bridges

Empathy:
Empathy doesn't erase differences, but it closes distance. It's the ability to imagine another's perspective without judgment. Bridges are built when understanding replaces assumption. Empathy shifts conflict into connection. Listening with care is often the strongest bridge you can build. Connection begins with empathy.

→ **Who could you build a bridge with today?**
Micro Challenge: Ask someone about their experience and listen fully.

Day 134: Boundaries Protect Focus

Boundaries:
Every distraction steals from your priorities. Boundaries are how you defend your attention. Without them, life pulls you in every direction. With them, you create space for what matters most. Focus thrives inside clear boundaries. Saying no is protecting your yes.

→ **What boundary could sharpen your focus today?**
Micro Challenge: Silence notifications during one focused work block.

Day 135: Curiosity Sparks Creativity

Curiosity:
Creativity doesn't appear from nowhere — it's born from curiosity. Asking fresh questions breaks open new ideas. Curiosity looks at the ordinary and wonders what else is possible. It turns routine into invention. Creativity grows where curiosity plays. Every new idea starts with a question.

→ **What could you get curious about today?**
Micro Challenge: Ask "what if" about one routine task.

Day 136: Gratitude Expands Joy

Gratitude:
Joy multiplies where gratitude lives. Focusing on blessings turns ordinary days into extraordinary ones. Gratitude doesn't wait for perfect circumstances — it finds light in shadows too. The more you practice it, the more joy you see. Gratitude changes perspective and mood. Joy grows through thanks.

→ **What joy could gratitude reveal today?**
Micro Challenge: Write down three things you're grateful for tonight.

Day 137: Grit Chooses Consistency

Grit:
Consistency beats talent, luck and mood. Grit is showing up again and again, even when progress feels slow. Each act of persistence compounds into strength. Excitement fades, but grit endures. The quiet decision to continue builds extraordinary results over time. Consistency is grit's gift.

→ **Where do you need consistency today?**
Micro Challenge: Do one repeat action for your long-term goal.

Day 138: Perspective Lifts the Load

Perspective:
A heavy problem can feel lighter with a shift in perspective. When you reframe it as training instead of punishment, strength grows. Perspective doesn't erase the weight, but it changes how you carry it. From another angle, struggle becomes shaping. Your story is shaped by your view.

→ **How could you reframe today's load?**
Micro Challenge: Write one sentence casting your challenge as growth.

Day 139: Growth Stretches Comfort

Growth:
Growth requires stepping outside the safe zone. Comfort may feel secure, but it limits progress. Every stretch feels awkward at first, but it expands your capacity. What feels uncomfortable now becomes your new normal later. Growth thrives in discomfort. Expansion lives beyond ease.

→ **Where could you stretch today?**
Micro Challenge: Take one action that feels just beyond your comfort zone.

Day 140: Reflection Clarifies Direction

Reflection:
Life gets noisy without reflection. Pausing helps you remember where you're going and why. Reflection filters out distractions and realigns priorities. It turns scattered effort into meaningful direction. The future becomes clearer when the past is reviewed. Reflection is clarity's foundation.

→ **What reflection could guide you today?**
Micro Challenge: Write down your top three priorities for the week.

Day 141: Focus Protects Progress

Focus:
Progress leaks through scattered effort. Focus keeps it contained and growing. Protecting attention from distractions ensures your steps count. Each focused moment compounds toward your goals. Without focus, work multiplies without meaning. Progress follows attention.

→ **What deserves your best focus today?**
Micro Challenge: Dedicate 30 distraction-free minutes to one task.

Day 142: Courage Breaks Patterns

Courage:
Patterns may feel safe but often keep you stuck. Courage disrupts them with change. Trying something new creates space for growth. Breaking routine takes bravery but builds freedom. Courage says, "This doesn't define me anymore." Patterns shift when courage acts.

→ **What pattern needs breaking today?**
Micro Challenge: Change one small habit in your routine.

Day 143: Resilience Adapts to Change

Resilience:
Change is constant, but resilience thrives in it. Fighting change wastes energy; adapting strengthens it. Resilience doesn't resist — it reshapes. Flexibility makes survival possible. Every adjustment proves your ability to endure. Strength grows when you bend, not break.

→ **Where could adaptability strengthen you today?**
Micro Challenge: Adjust one plan instead of forcing it.

Day 144: Discipline Shapes Destiny

Discipline:
Dreams inspire, but discipline delivers. Your destiny is formed by what you repeat daily. Each small habit becomes part of who you are becoming. Without discipline, destiny drifts; with it, direction solidifies. Big futures are built from small consistencies. Discipline is destiny in progress.

→ **What habit could shape your future today?**
Micro Challenge: Do one disciplined act tied to your long-term vision.

Day 145: Energy Follows Attention

Energy:
Your energy flows to what you focus on. Worry drains it, but purpose fuels it. Attention is the switch that directs your strength. Where your mind goes, energy follows. Choosing carefully means protecting capacity. Focus wisely and energy rises.

→ **Where is your energy flowing today?**
Micro Challenge: Redirect attention from worry to purposeful action.

Day 146: Relationships Thrive on Honesty

Relationships:
Honesty breathes life into relationships. Without it, trust weakens under pretence. With it, connection strengthens through clarity. Even difficult truths build stronger bonds when spoken with care. Real relationships require real words. Honesty is love's foundation.

→ **Who needs honesty from you today?**
Micro Challenge: Speak one truth kindly but clearly.

Day 147: Empathy Softens Conflict

Empathy:
Conflict hardens when no one feels understood. Empathy softens it by creating space for listening. It doesn't mean agreeing, but it does mean caring. Empathy transforms tension into respect. Relationships heal where empathy is practiced. Understanding eases division.

→ **Where could empathy soften tension today?**
Micro Challenge: Listen without interrupting and repeat back what you heard.

Day 148: Boundaries Guard Your Future

Boundaries:
Every yes shapes tomorrow. Boundaries protect your future from today's noise. Saying no now makes space for long-term yes. Without boundaries, tomorrow is consumed by distractions. With them, your vision stays intact. Boundaries are future protection.

→ **What boundary could protect tomorrow?**
Micro Challenge: Decline one demand that doesn't serve your future self.

Day 149: Curiosity Opens Connection

Curiosity:
People open up when you get curious about them. Questions show interest and care. Curiosity deepens conversations and builds trust. Assumptions divide; curiosity unites. Connection thrives where curiosity lives. Wonder builds closeness.

→ **Who could you get curious about today?**
Micro Challenge: Ask one thoughtful question you've never asked before.

Day 150: Gratitude Grounds You

Gratitude:
Gratitude steadies you when life feels chaotic. It anchors attention to what remains good. Even in storms, something holds. Gratitude brings calm by focusing on the steady. The more you practice, the stronger your balance. Gratitude grounds the soul.

→ **What holds you steady today?**
Micro Challenge: Write three things you can still count on.

Day 151: Grit Silences Excuses

Grit:
Excuses multiply when effort feels heavy. Grit outlasts them with persistence. Every act of endurance weakens their grip. Success often belongs to the one who stayed. Grit is action in the face of reason to quit. Excuses lose when grit holds.

→ **What excuse could you silence today?**
Micro Challenge: Take one step on something you've delayed.

May Workbook – Endurance Test

Endurance is not about speed, but about staying the course. This month challenged your patience, resilience and ability to keep moving when things grew heavy. Use this page to explore where endurance carried you and where it still needs strengthening.

1. Reflection

Where did I show endurance this month?

_____
_____
_____

What moments tested my patience or grit?

_____
_____
_____

How did gratitude make endurance easier?

_____
_____
_____

What mindset helped me keep going?

_____
_____
_____

What part of me feels stronger for it?

_____
_____
_____

2. Journaling Prompt

Complete this sentence: 'One step past comfort looks like…' Reflect on where that took you this month.

_____
_____
_____

3. Exercise

Create an 'Energy Budget.' Split a page into two lists: What drains me / What fuels me. Add at least three to each column. Circle one draining habit to reduce and one fuelling habit to increase.

[Use the space below to draw, sketch, or note your ideas.]

_____
_____
_____

June — Reflection

June marks the halfway point of the year. Six months behind you, six months ahead. It is a natural pause, a turning point, a place on the path where you stop for a moment to check the map. It is the perfect moment to reflect and to ask the questions that turn experience into wisdom. Without reflection, we keep moving but risk moving blindly. With reflection, every success and every mistake becomes a teacher that guides the steps to come.

Reflection is not about judgment. It is not about deciding if you're "behind" or "ahead." It is about noticing—with honesty and kindness—where you stand right now. Where have you grown stronger? What habits have taken root? Which ones slipped away without you noticing? Where have you drifted and what needs to be adjusted? Awareness is the first step to growth and June offers the light to see things clearly.

This month invites honesty, but also courage. Reflection may reveal uncomfortable truths: the routines you abandoned, the goals you've postponed, the limits you've quietly placed on yourself. That's okay. Reflection isn't defeat; it's direction. It doesn't shame you for where you are—it points toward where you want to go. The gift of June is clarity: a chance to choose your next six months with sharper focus.

But reflection isn't only about what's missing. It is also about gratitude. Look back at the victories, large and small. Notice the persistence you've shown, the resilience you've built, the courage you've practiced. Even the smallest wins are proof that you are stronger than yesterday. These wins are not accidents; they are the foundation you will carry into the rest of the year.

Practical reflection helps too. Write down your lessons. Capture the truths that surfaced in hard moments. Celebrate the patterns you want to repeat. Adjust the path where it's needed. A short pause now saves wasted miles later.

June is your mirror. Hold it up with steady hands. Look carefully. Be honest. Be kind. Then step forward with clarity. The story of this year is only half-written. What you choose now will shape the ending—and you get to decide how that ending reads.

Day 152: Perspective Creates Options

Perspective:
Problems look unsolvable when you stare too closely. Perspective shows new angles and hidden paths. Stepping back opens possibilities you couldn't see. The challenge may remain, but the options grow. Perspective is the door to creativity. Vision changes solutions.

→ **What other angle could you try today?**
Micro Challenge: Write down one alternative way forward.

Day 153: Growth Requires Risk

Growth:
Growth and safety don't coexist. To expand, you must risk failure, rejection, or discomfort. Each risk builds courage and skill. Avoiding risk avoids growth. Progress waits beyond fear. Risk is the price of growth.

→ **What risk could grow you today?**
Micro Challenge: Take one bold step you've been resisting.

Day 154: Reflection Gives Clarity

Reflection:
Without reflection, confusion multiplies. Pausing helps you see what matters and what doesn't. Reflection cuts through noise and creates focus. It gives direction to your next step. The future clears when you look back with honesty. Reflection is clarity's gift.

→ **What deserves reflection today?**
Micro Challenge: Spend five minutes journaling on your top lesson.

Day 155: Focus Simplifies Life

Focus:
Life feels heavy when everything feels urgent. Focus simplifies by naming the most important. When you focus, clutter falls away. Simplicity follows attention. The clearer your focus, the lighter your life. Focus lightens the load.

→ **What single task would simplify your day?**
Micro Challenge: Complete your top task before moving on.

Day 156: Courage is Trying Again

Courage:
Failure is not the end unless you refuse to try again. Courage is picking yourself up and giving it another go. Each retry weakens fear and strengthens confidence. Trying again builds resilience and humility. Courage is persistence with heart. Progress comes through repeated attempts.

→ **Where could you try again today?**
Micro Challenge: Restart one effort you've abandoned.

Day 157: Resilience Is Restarting

Resilience:
Falling isn't failure — refusing to restart is. Resilience is the ability to begin again. Each restart proves setbacks don't define you. It builds strength, humility and momentum. Progress isn't erased when you restart; it's reinforced. Resilience is starting again with wisdom.

→ **Where do you need to restart?**
Micro Challenge: Take the first step back into a dropped habit.

Day 158: Discipline Honors Promises

Discipline:
Promises to yourself shape identity. Discipline keeps them. Every kept promise builds trust; every broken one weakens it. Discipline proves your word matters. Over time, small commitments create unshakable belief. Self-respect grows through discipline. Promises honoured build identity.

→ **What promise could you honour today?**
Micro Challenge: Choose one small commitment and complete it fully.

Day 159: Energy Needs Rhythm

Energy:
Constant effort drains, but rhythm restores. Life has seasons of work, rest and play. Ignoring them leads to burnout. Respecting rhythm creates endurance. Energy thrives in cycles, not in constant push. Balance keeps strength alive.

→ **Where could rhythm restore your energy?**
Micro Challenge: Pause once today before resuming work.

Day 160: Relationships Need Presence

Relationships:
Presence is one of the rarest gifts in a distracted world. Being fully attentive communicates deep value. Even short moments of undivided attention strengthen connection. Absence weakens bonds, but presence restores them. Real connection is built in full attention. Presence is proof of love.

→ **Who deserves your full presence today?**
Micro Challenge: Have one conversation without any distractions.

Day 161: Empathy Deepens Connection

Empathy:
Empathy is the bridge between people. It allows you to step into another's world without judgment. When someone feels understood, walls come down and trust builds. Empathy doesn't demand agreement — only care. The more you practice it, the deeper your connections grow. Empathy is love in listening.

→ **Who could you connect with through empathy today?**
Micro Challenge: Ask one person how they're really doing and listen fully.

Day 162: Boundaries Guard Peace

Boundaries:
Peace doesn't just happen — it must be protected. Boundaries keep noise, stress and demands from overwhelming you. Without them, life feels chaotic; with them, you feel steady. Boundaries are not rejection but preservation. They guard your well-being so you can thrive. Peace is maintained by limits.

→ **What boundary could protect your peace today?**
Micro Challenge: Say no once today, calmly and clearly.

Day 163: Curiosity Strengthens Relationships

Curiosity:
Relationships grow when you show genuine curiosity. Asking thoughtful questions shows care and interest. Curiosity replaces assumption with understanding. It turns surface conversations into deeper connections. Bonds strengthen when people feel seen through your questions. Curiosity creates closeness.

→ **Who could you show curiosity toward today?**
Micro Challenge: Ask one meaningful question you've never asked before.

Day 164: Gratitude Softens Stress

Gratitude:
Stress narrows your focus to what's wrong. Gratitude widens it to include what's right. Even in difficult times, something remains steady. Gratitude doesn't erase stress but makes it lighter. The more you notice blessings, the easier it is to endure. Gratitude softens the weight of life.

→ **What blessing can you name today?**
Micro Challenge: Write down three good things before going to sleep.

Day 165: Grit Outlasts Obstacles

Grit:
Obstacles will appear in every journey. Grit is the decision to keep going anyway. Each step forward proves endurance is stronger than resistance. Over time, grit outlasts barriers until they break. Quitting makes obstacles permanent; persistence makes them temporary. Grit is victory in motion.

→ **Where could grit push you forward today?**
Micro Challenge: Take one step toward a goal despite resistance.

Day 166: Perspective Brings Balance

Perspective:
Life feels unbalanced when problems dominate your vision. Perspective restores balance by widening your view. Challenges are rarely the whole story — good often exists alongside struggle. A balanced outlook brings calm and clarity. Perspective doesn't remove problems, but it lightens them. Balance grows with vision.

→ **What else is true besides your struggle?**
Micro Challenge: Write three steady truths you can rely on today.

Day 167: Growth Demands Action

Growth:
Growth doesn't come from wishing — it comes from doing. Action moves you out of comfort and into progress. Even small steps compound into big change over time. Waiting keeps you still, but action builds momentum. Growth is action applied daily. Movement is the proof of progress.

→ **What action could grow you today?**
Micro Challenge: Take one step you've been delaying.

Day 168: Reflection Fuels Learning

Reflection:
Experience alone doesn't make you wiser. Reflection turns experience into learning. Pausing to review teaches what worked and what didn't. Reflection strengthens memory and meaning. Wisdom is reflection put into practice. Growth accelerates when you take time to reflect.

→ **What lesson deserves reflection today?**
Micro Challenge: Write one thing you learned this week.

Day 169: Focus Directs Energy

Focus:
Energy spreads thin without focus. By choosing one priority, you channel strength into impact. Scattered attention leads to exhaustion, while focused attention leads to progress. Focus is the director of your energy. Where your focus goes, growth follows. Focus makes power effective.

→ **What deserves your energy today?**
Micro Challenge: Block 30 minutes for your top priority.

Day 170: Courage Risks Rejection

Courage:
Rejection feels painful, but courage chooses to risk it. Avoiding rejection keeps you safe but small. Every bold attempt carries the chance of no — but also the chance of yes. Growth often hides on the other side of rejection. Courage accepts the risk for the reward. Bravery expands possibility.

→ **Where could you risk rejection today?**
Micro Challenge: Ask for one opportunity you've been hesitating on.

Day 171: Resilience Means Starting Over

Resilience:
Every setback invites a choice: stop or start again. Resilience chooses to start again, no matter how many times. Each restart proves you're stronger than the stumble. Beginning again isn't weakness — it's courage in action. Resilience is persistence reborn daily. Restarting is resilience at work.

→ **Where could you start over today?**
Micro Challenge: Restart one habit you've dropped recently.

Day 172: Discipline Builds Strength

Discipline:
Strength is forged in repetition. Discipline ensures you keep showing up, even when motivation fades. Each repeated action makes you stronger, inside and out. Discipline builds resilience by creating reliability. Over time, small acts of discipline accumulate into lasting power. Strength is consistency in motion.

→ **Where could discipline build strength today?**
Micro Challenge: Do one consistent action tied to your goal.

Day 173: Energy Grows Through Joy

Energy:
Joy isn't a distraction — it's fuel. Laughter, play and delight restore energy like nothing else. Without joy, life feels heavy and draining. Choosing joy lightens your load and recharges your spirit. Joy is not wasted time; it's renewal. Energy grows where joy is found.

→ **What joy could fuel you today?**
Micro Challenge: Do one activity that makes you smile.

Day 174: Relationships Require Repair

Relationships:
No relationship avoids tension. What matters is how you repair. Repair requires humility, honesty and effort. It transforms conflict into stronger connection. Avoidance makes cracks grow, but repair makes bonds resilient. Relationships thrive when repaired, not when ignored.

→ **Who could you begin repairing with today?**
Micro Challenge: Send one small message of care or apology.

Day 175: Empathy Invites Healing

Empathy:
Healing begins when someone feels seen. Empathy invites that healing by offering compassion instead of judgment. Listening with care creates safety for others to open up. You don't need answers — just presence. Empathy is the medicine of connection. Healing often begins in understanding.

→ **Who could you offer empathy to today?**
Micro Challenge: Let one person share without interruption.

Day 176: Boundaries Guard Freedom

Boundaries:
Boundaries don't trap you — they free you. By limiting what drains you, you create space for what matters most. Without boundaries, exhaustion takes over. With them, freedom flourishes. Boundaries are strength expressed with clarity. Freedom requires limits.

→ **What boundary could create freedom today?**
Micro Challenge: Say no once today to protect your time.

Day 177: Focus Reveals Priorities

Focus:
When everything feels urgent, nothing truly is. Focus cuts through noise and reveals what matters most. It's not about doing more but about doing what counts. Without focus, energy scatters into tasks that don't move you forward. With focus, priorities become clear and progress accelerates. Focus is the lens that sharpens life.

→ **What single priority deserves your attention today?**
Micro Challenge: Choose one task and complete it before starting anything else.

Day 178: Courage to Say No

Courage:
It's easier to say yes and harder to risk disappointment. But courage lies in protecting your time, energy and values with a clear no. Saying no honours what matters most. Each no creates space for your true yes. Courage isn't only in big battles; it's in small refusals too. Saying no is an act of strength.

→ **What no could free you today?**
Micro Challenge: Decline one request politely but firmly.

Day 179: Resilience Learns from Setbacks

Resilience:
Setbacks are part of every journey, but resilience turns them into teachers. Instead of asking "Why me?" ask "What now?" Resilience reframes failure as fuel for the future. Each bounce back strengthens character and confidence. Falling isn't the end — it's the classroom of endurance. Setbacks shape stronger comebacks.

→ **What setback is teaching you right now?**
Micro Challenge: Write one lesson you've gained from a recent setback.

Day 180: Discipline Keeps You Steady

Category: Discipline
Motivation comes and goes, but discipline steadies the course. It's the daily decision to act even when you don't feel like it. Discipline builds reliability with yourself. Each repeated action becomes part of who you are. When moods shift, discipline holds you steady. Progress is born from consistency.

→ **What discipline will keep you steady today?**
Micro Challenge: Commit to one routine action, no matter how you feel.

Day 181: Protect Your Energy

Energy:
Your energy is your fuel — without it, nothing moves. Protect it like the limited resource it is. Overcommitment and distraction drain it quickly. Protecting energy means saying no, resting and choosing wisely. A charged you is a better you. Energy guarded is energy gained.

→ **Where are you wasting energy unnecessarily?**
Micro Challenge: Remove one drain from your day and take a short rest.

June Workbook – Mid-Year Mirror

June marks the halfway point of the year — the perfect moment for reflection. Take stock of your progress, celebrate your wins and be honest about where you've drifted. Use this page as your mid-year mirror.

1. Reflection

What's my biggest win so far this year?

_____
_____
_____

What lesson keeps repeating itself?

_____
_____
_____

Where have I drifted from my goals?

_____
_____
_____

What am I most grateful for halfway through the year?

_____
_____
_____

What one change could make the next six months stronger?

_____

_____

_____

2. Journaling Prompt
Write a letter from your January self to your June self. What would past-you say about how far you've come?

_____

_____

_____

3. Exercise
Rate yourself (1–10) in: Focus, Energy, Discipline, Gratitude, Courage. For each score, write one action that could raise it by one point in the next month.

[Use the space below to draw, sketch, or note your ideas.]

_____

_____

_____

July — Courage

July brings boldness. The light is long, the days are full and courage finally asks for its turn. This is the month for daring steps—for saying what you've avoided saying, for trying what you've been afraid to attempt, for moving toward the version of yourself that only grows when fear is acknowledged but not obeyed.

Courage is not about fearlessness. It's about movement in spite of fear. Fear will always have its voice, always remind you of risks, always whisper reasons to stay small. Courage speaks softer but steadier. It says step forward anyway. It doesn't promise the outcome, but it does promise growth. July invites you to listen to that whisper and let it guide your choices.

This month may bring opportunities that stretch you. Don't wait for readiness—because readiness is rarely a feeling. It doesn't arrive wrapped neatly with certainty. Readiness is something you create through action. Each brave step builds evidence that you can and that evidence becomes confidence for the next leap. Even failure, when faced with courage, becomes fuel. It teaches you that the sting fades, the lesson remains and you are stronger for having dared.

Courage doesn't have to mean grand gestures. It can be small but significant: the honest conversation you've been postponing, the new project you've kept on the shelf, the boundary you've been afraid to set. Each act of courage clears space for more freedom.

And joy belongs here too. Courage is not always grim or heavy; it can be exhilarating. The very act of risk creates a spark, a sense of aliveness that comes only from stepping beyond comfort. Think of laughter that bursts after doing something you weren't sure you could do, the thrill of possibility discovered only because you said yes.

July's challenge is simple, though not easy: ask yourself, what would I do f I wasn't afraid? Then take one real, tangible step toward that answer. Write the email. Book the class. Speak the truth.

The season itself is bold—sun high, days stretched wide, life in full bloom. Match it. Step into courage. Let July remind you that bravery is not the absence of fear but the decision that fear does not get the final word.

Day 182: Small Acts Build Trust

Relationships:
Trust isn't built in grand moments but in small, repeated acts of care. Remembering details, checking in, showing up — these create safety. Consistency strengthens bonds more than intensity. Relationships grow strong one small act at a time. Every gesture counts.

→ **Who could use one small act of trust today?**
Micro Challenge: Send a thoughtful message or check-in to someone important.

Day 183: Empathy Softens Judgment

Empathy:
It's easy to judge someone's actions without knowing their story. Empathy slows you down and asks what they might be carrying. Understanding doesn't excuse behaviour, but it humanises the person. Empathy replaces judgment with compassion. It turns conflict into connection.

→ **Who could you see with more empathy today?**
Micro Challenge: Before reacting, imagine three challenges that person may face.

Day 184: Boundaries Build Freedom

Boundaries:
Boundaries aren't prisons — they're protection. They keep what matters safe from what doesn't. Without them, you end up stretched thin and resentful. With them, you preserve peace and create freedom. A clear no is often the doorway to your best yes. Boundaries give freedom shape.

→ **What boundary could you set today?**
Micro Challenge: Say no to one thing that doesn't align with your priorities.

Day 185: Curiosity Unlocks Growth

Curiosity:
Curiosity turns assumptions into discovery. By asking questions, you learn what you didn't know. Wonder keeps your mind alive and your world open. Curiosity fuels learning, connection and creativity. The more curious you are, the more possibilities appear. Curiosity unlocks growth where certainty stalls.

→ **What question could open a door today?**
Micro Challenge: Ask one "what if" question in an area you feel stuck.

Day 186: Gratitude Balances Pressure

Gratitude:
Pressure focuses on what's missing or at risk. Gratitude balances it by naming what's already here. Even under stress, there is always something steady to count. Gratitude doesn't remove problems, but it makes them lighter. Counting blessings steadies your heart under weight. Gratitude is strength disguised as softness.

→ **What can you be grateful for in this pressure?**
Micro Challenge: Write down three things that are still steady today.

Day 187: Grit Keeps Showing Up

Grit:
Success isn't built in bursts but in steady return. Grit is showing up again and again, especially when motivation fades. It's the decision to continue when others quit. Over time, grit outlasts talent and opportunity. Progress belongs to those who keep returning. Grit is consistency with teeth.

→ **Where do you need grit today?**
Micro Challenge: Do one small action in the place you feel like giving up.

Day 188: Perspective Shrinks Problems

Perspective:
Problems can feel massive when you're too close to them. Perspective zooms out and reminds you of the bigger picture. Most struggles are smaller than they feel in the moment. Stepping back gives proportion and clarity. With perspective, problems become challenges you can handle. Vision changes the weight.

→ **What would this problem look like a year from now?**
Micro Challenge: Write one sentence reframing your current challenge as temporary.

Day 189: Growth Is a Choice

Growth:
Growth doesn't just happen — it's chosen. You can stay safe in comfort or step into discomfort that stretches you. Each choice shapes who you become. Growth begins with small risks that expand capacity. Repeated over time, they transform you. Choosing growth is choosing a bigger life.

→ **What choice today could grow you?**
Micro Challenge. Do one task that feels uncomfortable but valuable.

Day 190: Reflection Builds Wisdom

Reflection:
Experience alone doesn't create wisdom — reflection does. Without pause, lessons slip by unnoticed. Reflection slows you down to see patterns and extract meaning. Looking back turns mistakes into teachers and successes into guides. Reflection strengthens the path forward. Wisdom grows when you pause.

→What moment deserves reflection today?
Micro Challenge: Write three lines about what you've learned this week.

Day 191: Focus Demands Boundaries

Focus:
Focus is impossible without boundaries. Distractions creep in and steal attention if you let them. Guarding your focus requires defending your time and space. Boundaries protect priorities from interruptions. Focus grows in protected zones. Guard your yes with strong no's.

→ What focus boundary could you set today?
Micro Challenge: Turn off notifications during one work block.

Day 192: Courage Breaks Patterns

Courage:
Patterns feel safe but keep you stuck. Courage interrupts them by trying something new. Change is uncomfortable, but it creates growth. Courage is choosing disruption over repetition. Every broken pattern is a step toward freedom. Bold choices create new paths.

→ **What pattern needs breaking today?**
Micro Challenge: Try one small change in your usual routine.

Day 193: Resilience Means Rest

Resilience:
Pushing without pause isn't strength — it's strain. Resilience grows through recovery as much as effort. Rest restores energy so you can continue. Without it, you burn out instead of build up. Rest is part of the plan, not the failure of it. Resilience knows when to stop.

→ **Where do you need to rest for resilience?**
Micro Challenge: Schedule 15 minutes of intentional rest today.

Day 194: Discipline Shapes Character

Discipline
Character isn't built in grand decisions but in daily discipline. Each act of consistency forms your identity. Over time, your choices define you more than your intentions. Discipline is the bridge between values and behaviour. It creates the character you respect. Small actions, repeated, shape the person you become.

→ **What discipline could shape your character today?**
Micro Challenge: Do one action that reflects your values clearly.

Day 195: Energy Needs Renewal

Energy:
Energy drains with use, but it also restores with care. Renewal is not optional; it's essential. Without it, you collapse under strain. Renewal can be rest, play, nature, or connection. Choose renewal often and your energy deepens. Renewal is fuel for tomorrow's strength.

→ **What renewal could refuel you today?**
Micro Challenge: Spend 10 minutes on something that restores you.

Day 196: Relationships Need Repair

Relationships:
Conflict and distance happen in every relationship. What matters is repair. Avoidance deepens cracks, but honest effort heals them. Repair requires humility, patience and presence. Strong relationships aren't conflict-free; they're built on repair. Repair is proof of love in action.

→ **Who could you repair with today?**
Micro Challenge: Reach out with one word of care or apology.

Day 197: Empathy Creates Connection

Empathy:
True connection comes when people feel seen and understood. Empathy creates that connection by listening with openness. It doesn't require fixing, just presence. Empathy says, "I'm with you" instead of "I'll solve you." People don't forget being understood. Connection grows where empathy lives.

→ **Who could use your empathy today?**
Micro Challenge: Ask someone how they're feeling and listen fully.

Day 198: Boundaries Build Respect

Boundaries:
Boundaries aren't selfish; they teach others how to treat you. When you honour your limits, people learn to honour them too. Respect grows from clarity, not from over giving. Boundaries strengthen trust in relationships. They say: this is where I stand and this is how we can walk together.

→ **What boundary would earn respect today?**
Micro Challenge: State one clear limit calmly and without apology.

Day 199: Curiosity Sparks Creativity

Curiosity:
Creativity often starts with curiosity. Asking new questions leads to new solutions. Wonder breaks the pattern of "how it's always been." Curiosity is the seed of innovation. The more questions you ask, the more ideas you grow. Creativity thrives where curiosity plays.

→ **What could you get curious about today?**
Micro Challenge: Ask "what if" about one routine task.

Day 200: Gratitude Multiplies Joy

Gratitude:
Joy grows where gratitude is practiced. Gratitude shifts your attention from lack to abundance. Small thank yous turn ordinary moments into treasures. Gratitude doesn't wait for perfect conditions — it finds good in what's already here. The more you notice, the more joy multiplies. Gratitude is joy in action.

→ **What can you thank today?**
Micro Challenge: Write down three things that made you smile.

Day 201: Grit Outlasts Doubt

Grit:
Doubt whispers reasons to quit. Grit outlasts those whispers with steady steps. Each act of perseverance weakens doubt's voice. Over time, grit proves stronger than uncertainty. Success often belongs to the ones who simply stayed longer. Grit is doubt's undoing.

→ **Where do you need grit to outlast doubt?**
Micro Challenge: Do one task you've been postponing due to uncertainty.

Day 202: Perspective Restores Peace

Perspective:
Stress grows when problems take up your whole vision. Perspective restores peace by widening the frame. Seeing the bigger picture shrinks panic and creates calm. Often, the challenge is smaller than it feels right now. Perspective changes how you carry the load. A wider view makes a lighter heart.

→ **What wider view could restore peace for you today?**
Micro Challenge: Write down one reason this challenge is temporary.

Day 203: Growth Requires Risk

Growth:
Growth and safety rarely coexist. Risk stretches you into new spaces. Without it, progress stalls. Each risk teaches courage and skill. Growth is the reward for stepping into uncertainty. Safe paths rarely lead to bigger selves.

→ **What risk could grow you today?**
Micro Challenge: Take one small step you've avoided out of fear.

Day 204: Reflection Brings Direction

Reflection:
Without reflection, it's easy to drift through days without purpose. Pausing helps you ask where you're going and why. Reflection realigns you with what matters most. It saves you from chasing everything and missing the important things. Clarity is born in quiet. Reflection is how you steer.

→ **Where could reflection give you direction?**
Micro Challenge: Write down your top three priorities for this week.

Day 205: Focus Simplifies Life

Focus:
Life feels overwhelming when everything matters equally. Focus simplifies by naming what truly matters and letting the rest wait. Clarity grows when you protect attention for essentials. Doing less with depth brings better results. Simplicity is the reward of focus. Focus lightens life.

→ **What one thing would simplify your day if done first?**
Micro Challenge: Identify and complete that one thing today.

Day 206: Courage Begins Small

Courage:
Courage isn't always dramatic — sometimes it's tiny steps. Speaking up, trying again, or showing up can be acts of bravery. Small courage builds confidence for bigger challenges. Every brave act, no matter how small, strengthens your character. Courage is a muscle that grows with use. Start where you are.

→ **Where could you practice small courage today?**
Micro Challenge: Take one tiny action that feels a little scary.

Day 207: Resilience Is Restarting

Resilience:
Resilience is the decision to begin again after falling. Everyone stumbles, but not everyone restarts. Each restart builds strength and humility. Restarting proves failure isn't final. Resilience grows every time you choose to continue. Beginning again is an act of power.

→ **Where do you need to restart?**
Micro Challenge: Take one first step back into a goal you've dropped.

Day 208: Discipline Honors Promises

Discipline:
Promises to others matter but promises to yourself shape identity. Discipline is how you keep them. Each kept promise strengthens self-trust; each broken one weakens it. Discipline proves you can rely on yourself. Over time, that trust becomes confidence. Honor begins with discipline.

→ **What promise will you keep today?**
Micro Challenge: Choose one small commitment and complete it without fail.

Day 209: Focus Filters the Noise

Focus:
The world is noisy — notifications, opinions and distractions compete for your mind. Without a filter, your attention scatters and progress stalls. Focus acts as that filter, cutting through noise and revealing what truly matters. By ignoring the unnecessary, you give your best energy to the essential. Clarity isn't found in doing more but in doing what counts. Focus is the art of choosing wisely.

→ **What noise could you filter out today?**
Micro Challenge: Turn off one source of distraction for two hours.

Day 210: Courage is Honesty

Courage:
Honesty requires courage because it exposes you. Speaking truth risks rejection or conflict, but it builds trust and clarity. Dishonesty may protect you briefly but erodes relationships long term. Courage chooses truth, even when it feels uncomfortable. The strongest bonds are built on honesty. Truth spoken with care strengthens everything it touches.

→ **Where do you need courage to be honest today?**
Micro Challenge: Speak one truth with kindness but without compromise.

Day 211: Resilience Adjusts the Pace

Resilience:
Resilience isn't running at full speed all the time. It's knowing when to push forward, when to slow down and when to rest. Pacing yourself wisely ensures you last for the long journey. Burnout is often the result of refusing to pause. Resilience honours rhythm and endurance. Adjusting pace is wisdom, not weakness.

→ **Where could adjusting your pace strengthen resilience?**
Micro Challenge: Remove or delay one non-essential task today.

Day 212: Discipline Aligns Actions

Discipline:
Discipline isn't about restriction; it's about alignment. Each choice either moves you closer to your values or away from them. Discipline ensures your daily actions reflect who you want to be. Without it, you drift and lose trust in yourself. With it, you create confidence and clarity. Alignment through discipline builds integrity.

→ **Where could discipline align your choices today?**
Micro Challenge: Choose one value and act in line with it today.

July Workbook – Acts of Courage

Courage isn't the absence of fear — it's action in spite of it. July tested your willingness to step into the unknown, to try, to risk and to grow. Use this page to acknowledge where you showed courage and where you can be bolder still.

1. Reflection
Where did I act bravely this month?

_____
_____
_____

Where did fear hold me back?

_____
_____
_____

What risks changed me for the better?

_____
_____
_____

What moments proved I was stronger than I thought?

_____
_____
_____

What's the next step that scares me?

_____
_____
_____

2. Journaling Prompt
Write on this: 'If I was bolder, I would…' Let yourself imagine freely, without holding back.

_____
_____
_____

3. Exercise
Draw a 'Fear Ladder.' Start with one small fear on the bottom rung, building up to a bigger one at the top. Choose one rung to tackle next month.

[Use the space below to draw, sketch, or note your ideas.]

_____
_____
_____

August — Resilience

August tests endurance in a different way. The heat lingers, fatigue builds and routine begins to feel like weight. Progress, once energising, can start to drag. This is the month where resilience steps to the front. Endurance got you moving. Resilience keeps you standing.

Resilience is not about never falling. It's about rising again. It's about adapting, recovering and continuing when setbacks arrive. And setbacks will come—interrupted schedules, unexpected demands, dips in energy, days that feel heavier than they should. None of this is a sign of failure; it is the texture of life. The question is never if challenges appear, but how you choose to respond when they do.

Recovery is part of resilience. Rest is not weakness; it's rebuilding. A strong tree bends in the storm; it does not snap. Resilience knows when to bend, when to pause and when to conserve strength for tomorrow. This month, honour your limits. Protect your energy with boundaries. Rest when needed, fuel well and allow quiet spaces. True resilience is not constant motion—it's sustainable motion.

Resilience also reframes. It sees setbacks not as proof of failure but as proof of movement. A stumble means you were walking. A restart means you're still willing. Each delay is not an ending but a chance to learn. Ask: What is this moment teaching me? How can I carry the lesson forward? That shift of perspective transforms obstacles into stepping stones.

August is not about perfection. It's about persistence with wisdom. It's about recognising that sometimes strength looks like pressing on and sometimes it looks like resting deliberately so you can return stronger. Both are valid. Both are powerful.

When the days feel long and the work feels heavy, remind yourself: you've risen before and you will rise again. Every restart is a declaration that you are still here, still moving, still becoming. That is resilience.

So let August be a teacher. Let it test you, not to break you, but to reveal how much stronger you've become since the year began. Meet the weight with patience, meet the heat with calm and meet the setbacks with steady resolve. Resilience isn't glamorous—but it will carry you through.

Day 213: Energy Needs Renewal

Energy:
Energy isn't endless — it must be renewed. Rest, laughter and quiet moments restore what constant doing drains. Ignoring renewal creates exhaustion that no amount of effort can fix. Renewal isn't indulgence; it's survival. Protecting your energy ensures you can keep going. Refuelling is a strength, not a weakness.

→ **What renewal could recharge you today?**
Micro Challenge: Take 15 minutes for something that restores you.

Day 214: Relationships Grow with Consistency

Relationships:
Relationships don't thrive on occasional gestures — they thrive on steady care. Consistency builds trust far more than intensity. People remember how often you show up, not just how grandly. Daily signals of value keep bonds strong. Connection grows in repeated actions of care. Consistency is proof of love.

→ **Who needs your consistency today?**
Micro Challenge: Check in with one person you often overlook.

Day 215: Empathy = Understanding

Empathy:
Empathy isn't about fixing — it's about listening. People open up when they feel understood. Understanding doesn't mean agreement; it means respect. Empathy turns conflict into connection and judgment into compassion. It creates safety where walls once stood. Connection grows with empathy.

→ **Who could you understand better today?**
Micro Challenge: Ask someone about their experience and listen fully.

Day 216: Boundaries Protect Peace

Boundaries:
Peace requires limits. Without boundaries, noise, stress and demands invade your space. Boundaries are not selfish — they are essential. They guard what matters most from being consumed. Every no protects your deeper yes. Boundaries are the foundation of peace.

→ **What boundary could protect your peace today?**
Micro Challenge: Say no once today to something unnecessary.

Day 217: Curiosity Unlocks Growth

Curiosity:
Curiosity asks, "What else is possible?" It replaces assumption with exploration. Without curiosity, growth stalls; with it, new paths appear. Curiosity fuels learning, creativity and connection. The more you ask, the more you see. Growth thrives where curiosity lives.

→ **What question could open growth today?**
Micro Challenge: Ask one new question in a place you feel stuck.

Day 218: Gratitude Reframes Pressure

Gratitude:
Pressure makes you see only what's missing. Gratitude balances it by noticing what's already steady. Even in stress, something remains good. Gratitude doesn't remove pressure but makes it lighter. Focusing on blessings creates resilience. Gratitude changes the story you tell yourself.

→ **What blessing could you name in your pressure?**
Micro Challenge: Write three things still working in your favour.

Day 219: Grit Outlasts Doubt

Grit:
Doubt whispers reasons to quit. Grit answers with persistence. Progress belongs to those who endure longer than their fear. Every act of showing up weakens doubt's grip. Grit is not flashy but steady. Doubt fades when grit holds.

→ **Where do you need grit today?**
Micro Challenge: Take one step forward despite uncertainty.

Day 220: Perspective Lightens the Load

Perspective:
Problems feel heavier when they dominate your vision. Perspective pulls you back to see the bigger story. Struggles are often smaller when viewed alongside the whole of life. Perspective doesn't remove weight but changes how you carry it. Calm returns when vision expands.

→ **How could perspective lighten your burden today?**
Micro Challenge: Write one sentence framing your challenge as temporary.

Day 221: Growth Comes Through Discomfort

Growth:
Comfort zones protect you but keep you small. Discomfort signals growth is happening. Each step into the unfamiliar stretches your capacity. What feels awkward today becomes strength tomorrow. Discomfort is not danger — it's expansion in progress. Growth always lives beyond comfort.

→ **Where could discomfort help you grow today?**
Micro Challenge: Do one task that feels slightly uncomfortable.

Day 222: Reflection Creates Clarity

Reflection:
Without reflection, life feels chaotic and repetitive. Pausing reveals patterns and lessons. Reflection turns mistakes into teachers and successes into guides. It clarifies direction and strengthens decisions. Wisdom comes from looking back before moving forward. Reflection is clarity in motion.

→ **What deserves reflection today?**
Micro Challenge: Write down one lesson you've learned this week.

Day 223: Focus Simplifies Life

Focus:
Life feels overwhelming when everything matters equally. Focus simplifies by highlighting what's essential. Doing less with depth creates more progress than doing more with distraction. Simplicity is the reward of focus. The clearer your focus, the lighter your life feels.

→ **What one focus would simplify your day?**
Micro Challenge: Protect 30 minutes for your most important task.

Day 224: Courage Faces Fear

Courage:
Fear tempts you to delay, but courage moves anyway. Waiting for fear to disappear keeps you stuck. Each act of courage shrinks fear's power. Bravery is not the absence of fear but action despite it. Courage grows stronger in motion. Fear weakens when faced.

→ **What fear could you face today?**
Micro Challenge: Take one action you've been avoiding.

Day 225: Resilience Finds Strength in Rest

Resilience:
Resilience isn't only about pushing forward — it's also about knowing when to pause. Rest restores the strength that effort drains. Without it, endurance turns into exhaustion. Taking a break doesn't mean giving up; it means preparing to go further. Rest is the hidden partner of resilience. True strength knows how to recover.

→ **Where could rest make you more resilient today?**
Micro Challenge: Schedule 15 minutes of intentional rest.

Day 226: Discipline Builds Self-Trust

Discipline:
Self-trust is built by doing what you said you'd do. Discipline ensures your actions match your words. Each kept promise strengthens confidence in yourself. Without discipline, belief weakens; with it, self-trust grows. Discipline proves you can count on you. Trust is earned daily.

→ **What promise could you honour today?**
Micro Challenge: Keep one commitment to yourself before the day ends.

Day 227: Energy Grows Through Renewal

Energy:
Energy drains with effort, but it renews with care. Renewal comes through sleep, play, nature and joy. Without it, strength collapses; with it, endurance builds. Renewal isn't optional — it's essential. Protecting your energy means choosing to recharge. Renewal is fuel for resilience.

→ **What renewal could fuel you today?**
Micro Challenge: Do one activity that restores you.

Day 228: Relationships Require Repair

Relationships:
Every relationship experiences strain. What matters is whether you repair. Avoidance creates distance, but honest effort rebuilds trust. Repair takes humility, care and patience. Strong relationships are not conflict-free; they're resilient through repair. Love is proven in how you mend.

→ **Who could you repair with today?**
Micro Challenge: Reach out with one word of care or apology.

Day 229: Empathy Strengthens Bonds

Empathy:
Empathy makes people feel valued and understood. When you listen with compassion, connection deepens. You don't have to fix everything — sometimes presence is enough. Empathy transforms judgment into trust. Relationships grow strong where empathy is practiced. Bonds are strengthened through care.

→ **Who could use your empathy today?**
Micro Challenge: Ask one person how they're really feeling and listen fully.

Day 230: Boundaries Guard Energy

Boundaries:
Every yes costs energy. Boundaries protect your fuel by ensuring you don't give it all away. Without them, you burn out; with them, you stay strong. Saying no isn't rejection — it's protection. Boundaries keep your best energy for your best work. Limits are strength in action.

→ **What boundary could protect your energy today?**
Micro Challenge: Say no once to preserve your strength.

Day 231: Curiosity Sparks Discovery

Curiosity:
Discovery begins with curiosity. By asking questions, you see what others overlook. Curiosity opens doors where assumptions build walls. It fuels creativity and learning every day. Wonder keeps life fresh and alive. Curiosity is the path to discovery.

→ **What could curiosity uncover for you today?**
Micro Challenge: Ask one new question about something ordinary.

Day 232: Gratitude Strengthens Perspective

Gratitude:
Perspective shifts when you focus on what's steady and good. Gratitude widens your lens and lightens your load. It doesn't erase challenges but balances them with blessings. Gratitude reminds you that not everything is wrong. The more you count, the more peace you feel. Perspective grows with gratitude.

→ **What can you thank today?**
Micro Challenge: Write three things you're grateful for before bed.

Day 233: Grit Stays When It's Boring

Grit:
Excitement fades quickly, but grit endures. Progress is often built in boring, unseen moments. Showing up when it's dull creates strength most people never develop. Grit is the decision to persist without applause. Endurance in silence leads to visible success later. Quiet consistency wins.

→ **Where do you need grit today?**
Micro Challenge: Work five more minutes on a task you'd rather drop.

Day 234: Perspective Restores Peace

Perspective:
Problems grow larger when you stare only at them. Perspective zooms out and reminds you of the bigger story. Most struggles are temporary chapters, not the whole book. Peace returns when you see beyond today. Perspective doesn't erase pain, but it eases it. Vision creates calm.

→ **What wider view could restore peace today?**
Micro Challenge: Write one sentence framing your challenge as temporary.

Day 235: Growth is a Daily Choice

Growth:
Growth doesn't arrive all at once — it happens daily. Every decision is a vote for the person you're becoming. Small steps compound into transformation. Growth requires intention and courage each day. Waiting for the right moment delays progress. Choosing growth today builds tomorrow's strength.

→ **What choice could grow you today?**
Micro Challenge: Take one action that stretches you out of comfort.

Day 236: Reflection Builds Direction

Reflection:
Direction doesn't come from rushing but from reflecting. Reflection slows you down to see where you're heading and why. Without it, you drift and waste energy on what doesn't matter. With it, priorities sharpen and choices simplify. Reflection is how you steer. Clarity grows when you pause.

→ **What deserves reflection today?**
Micro Challenge: Write your top three priorities for the week.

Day 237: Focus Creates Progress

Focus:
Progress isn't about speed — it's about attention. Scattered effort moves in circles, while focused effort moves forward. Concentrating on one step creates momentum for the next. Focus ensures your work matters. The sharper your focus, the faster your progress. Attention builds movement.

→ **What deserves your focus most today?**
Micro Challenge: Block 30 minutes for your top task.

Day 238: Courage Tries Again

Courage:
Failure is not the end unless you stop trying. Courage gives you strength to begin again. Each retry builds resilience and confidence. Trying again shows that setbacks don't define you. Courage isn't about never falling — it's about rising repeatedly. Bravery is persistence with heart.

→ **Where do you need to try again today?**
Micro Challenge: Restart one action you've recently dropped.

Day 239: Resilience Chooses Patience

Resilience:
Resilience isn't just endurance — it's patience. Not every struggle ends quickly. Waiting without giving up is strength in itself. Patience helps you last until the breakthrough arrives. Each day of waiting grows character and steadiness. Resilience is holding on with hope.

→ **Where could patience help you today?**
Micro Challenge: Take three slow breaths before responding to stress.

Day 240: Discipline Builds Legacy

Discipline:
Legacy isn't built in grand gestures but in daily habits. What you repeat shapes who you become and who you become shapes what you leave behind. Discipline creates that repetition. Without it, legacies fade. With it, your life tells a consistent story. Discipline is legacy in motion,

→ **What daily discipline could shape your legacy?**
Micro Challenge:
Choose one habit that reflects the person you want to be remembered as. Do it today.

Day 241: Aim the Beam

Focus:
Your attention is like a beam of light: spread wide, it's weak; narrowed, it's powerful. Scattered effort looks busy but delivers little. Focus means choosing one aim and ignoring the rest, even when they clamour for attention. When you protect that beam, you make progress where it counts instead of everywhere at once.

→ **What single priority deserves your full beam today?**
Micro Challenge: Block 30 minutes and do only one task without switching.

Day 242: Say the Scary Thing

Courage:
Fear grows in silence but shrinks when spoken. The sentence you're avoiding carries both risk and relief. Honesty said with kindness clears the air, even if your voice shakes. Courage isn't about being fearless; it's about being truthful despite fear. On the other side of expression is freedom and strength. Saying the scary thing makes space for trust.

→ **What truth have you been holding back?**
Micro Challenge: Speak one honest line today, calmly and clearly.

Day 243: Flex to Last

Resilience:
Resilience isn't rigid toughness; it's flexible endurance. Trees that bend in storms survive longer than those that refuse to move. Adapting timelines, tactics, or expectations isn't weakness — it's strategy. Stubbornness can break you, but flexibility keeps you in the game. Resilience is knowing when to bend and when to stand tall. That balance keeps you moving forward.

→ **Where could flexibility help you endure?**
Micro Challenge: Adjust one expectation today by loosening it 20%.

August Workbook – Resilience Reset

August asked you to bend without breaking, to adapt when things didn't go as planned. Resilience isn't about avoiding setbacks — it's about finding your footing again and again. Use this page to explore how resilience shaped your month.

1. Reflection

Where did I bend but not break this month?

_____
_____
_____

What setbacks did I recover from?

_____
_____
_____

How did I adapt to changes?

_____
_____
_____

What inner strength surprised me?

_____
_____
_____

What will I carry forward into September?

_____
_____
_____

2. Journaling Prompt
Write about one challenge that tested you but ultimately taught you something valuable.

_____
_____
_____

3. Exercise
Draw two timelines: 'What I planned' vs. 'What actually happened.' Highlight the differences. Mark the points where resilience carried you through.

[Use the space below to draw, sketch, or note your ideas.]

_____
_____
_____

September — Focus

September is a month of clarity. The rush of summer fades, routines return and the year begins its final arc. Where August asked for resilience, September asks for refinement. Focus becomes the theme.

Distractions will multiply as responsibilities stack up—work, school schedules, shifting seasons and unfinished goals competing for your attention. Focus is the way through. It is not about doing more; it is about cutting through noise. This month invites you to refine priorities, to strip away what no longer serves and to channel your energy where it will count most.

Perspective supports focus. Step back and ask: Why did I begin this journey? What matters most to me now? When purpose is clear, focus sharpens naturally. Without purpose, everything feels urgent. With purpose, urgency falls away and only what truly matters remains. Let September be the month where you remember your "why" and allow it to guide your "what."

September also offers a quiet reset. Summer may have pulled you off course—late nights, shifting routines, or moments of drift. That's okay. Drift is part of the cycle. What matters is the return. This is the time to realign, to bring discipline back to the forefront and to set yourself on a steady path for the final stretch of the year. Clarity doesn't demand perfection; it simply asks for honesty and intention.

Practical focus requires boundaries. Protect your mornings. Guard your time. Reduce clutter in both your environment and your commitments. Write down the three things that truly move you forward each day and give them your best effort before tending to anything else. Focus flourishes when energy is directed rather than scattered.

And remember, focus doesn't just produce progress—it produces peace. When your attention is divided, life feels chaotic. When you concentrate on fewer things with deeper intent, life feels calmer, even in the midst of demands. Clarity simplifies and simplicity strengthens.

September is your reminder: clarity is power. Let it guide you like a compass. Strip away the distractions, reclaim your purpose and carry that sharpened focus into the final months of the year. What you refine now will define how you finish.

Day 244: Protect the Battery

Energy:
Energy is your most valuable resource, yet it's the one most often wasted. Like a phone, you can't run on empty forever. Protecting energy means deciding what gets a share and what doesn't. When the battery is healthy, everything else runs better. Guard it like your life depends on it — because it does.

→ **Where are you leaking energy unnecessarily?**
Micro Challenge: Say no once and schedule a 10-minute recharge.

Day 245: Small Signals, Strong Ties

Relationships:
Strong bonds aren't built on grand gestures but on repeated small signals of care. A quick check-in, a remembered detail, or a kind note has lasting impact. Waiting for the "perfect time" to connect often means never connecting. Consistency builds trust more than occasional intensity. Small, steady signals grow into sturdy ties. Relationships thrive when tended daily.

→ **Who could use a brief reminder you care today?**
Micro Challenge: Send a two-line message with one specific appreciation.

Day 246: Look Under the Surface

Empathy:
Behaviour is only the tip of the iceberg. Hidden pressures drive much of what people do. Empathy means delaying judgment long enough to ask why. It doesn't excuse poor behaviour, but it adds humanity to the person. When you look underneath, conflict softens and understanding grows. Compassion starts there.

→ **Whose actions deserve a second look today?**
Micro Challenge: Imagine three possible stressors they might be under.

Day 247: Guard the Gate

Boundaries:
Every yes spends a portion of your limited energy and time. Without boundaries, your most important priorities get buried under lesser tasks. Guarding the gate means deciding what enters and what doesn't. Saying no isn't selfish; it's essential to protect your best yes. The gate is yours to hold.

→ **What no would protect your best yes today?**
Micro Challenge: Decline one nonessential request firmly but kindly.

Day 248: Ask a Better Question

Curiosity:
Assumptions close doors, but questions open them. Curiosity refreshes problems that feel stale and creates paths that weren't visible before. A single "What if?" or "How else?" can shift everything. Curiosity doesn't need all the answers — it simply invites possibility. The right question can reveal the opportunity hiding in plain sight. Keep asking until the way forward appears.

→ **What question could change this stuck spot?**
Micro Challenge: Ask one new question today — of yourself or someone else.

Day 249: Gratitude in Motion

Gratitude:
Gratitude doesn't erase challenges, but it balances them with perspective. Naming what's steady makes burdens lighter and patience stronger. Gratitude is less about feelings and more about attention. When you focus on what's good, more good comes into view. It steadies you in storms and softens the climb. Gratitude is strength disguised as softness.

→ **What's quietly good right now?**
Micro Challenge: Write down three things already working in your life today.

Day 250: Stay One More Rep

Grit:
Most people quit at the edge of discomfort, just before growth begins. Grit is choosing to stay longer, to endure the boring middle when excitement fades. That persistence compounds over time into mastery and results. The extra rep proves to yourself that you can last. Grit isn't glamorous — but it's powerful.

→ **Where can you stay five minutes longer today?**
Micro Challenge: Push past the urge to stop by one small step.

Day 251: Change the Angle

Perspective:
Problems can feel overwhelming when you're too close. A shift in angle often reveals they're smaller than they seem. Perspective doesn't change reality, but it changes your ability to face it. Viewing something as training instead of punishment lightens the load. Stepping back shows you options hidden in plain sight. The angle you choose shapes the strength you feel.

→ **How would your future self-see this?**
Micro Challenge: Rewrite your challenge as training in one sentence.

Day 252: Choose the Stretch

Growth:
Growth doesn't happen by accident; it's chosen through stretch. Comfort zones feel safe but keep you small. Every small discomfort you embrace expands your capacity. Over time, today's stretch becomes tomorrows normal. Stretch enough times and you find yourself stronger than you thought. Growth loves the edges of discomfort.

→ **What stretch will you choose today?**
Micro Challenge: Take the smallest uncomfortable step forward now.

Day 253: Clear the Clutter

Reflection:
Clutter isn't only physical — it's mental, emotional and digital too. When too much piles up, clarity disappears. Reflection helps you notice what's noise and what's necessary. By clearing clutter, you create space for focus and calm. Progress often begins with subtraction, not addition. A lighter load helps you move further.

→ **What clutter could you clear right now?**
Micro Challenge: Write down one thing to release today and act on it.

Day 254: Narrow the Spotlight

Focus:
Attention scattered across too many things loses power. By narrowing the spotlight, you put energy where it counts. Single tasking may feel slow, but it produces real progress. Multitasking creates motion, not results. Focus is how you trade busyness for effectiveness. What you spotlight grows stronger.

→ **Where could you shine a single spotlight today?**
Micro Challenge: Pick one task and complete it before moving to the next.

Day 255: Step Into the Risk

Courage:
Risk feels dangerous because it threatens certainty. Yet every meaningful step forward requires it. Playing safe keeps you stable but stagnant. Courage is choosing risk with intention, trusting growth will follow. Fear may still walk beside you, but it doesn't have to lead. Risk is often the price of breakthrough.

→ **What risk is worth taking today?**
Micro Challenge: Do one thing uncertain — even if the step is tiny.

Day 256: Bounce Back Quicker

Resilience:
Resilience isn't about never falling — it's about how quickly you rise again. The gap between setback and restart defines your strength. Shortening that gap builds confidence and momentum. Every quick bounce back teaches you that failure isn't final. The faster you stand, the less power the stumble has. Falling is natural; rising is chosen.

→ Where could you restart today instead of waiting?
Micro Challenge: Pick one dropped habit and restart it before tonight.

Day 257: Discipline is Freedom

Discipline:
Structure looks restrictive, but it frees you from constant decision-making. When routines hold, energy is saved for what matters most. Discipline trades chaos for clarity. Without it, you're at the mercy of moods and impulses. With it, you live by design, not default. Freedom flows from structure well kept.

→ Where could discipline free you right now?
Micro Challenge: Follow one small routine today with zero compromise.

Day 258: Energy Grows by Giving

Energy
Energy multiplies when shared with others. Encouraging words, small kindness, or genuine presence lift both giver and receiver. Contribution fuels vitality in ways comfort cannot. Withholding drains you, giving recharges you. Energy isn't only protected — it's created in connection. Sharing sparks strength.

→ **Who could you energise today?**
Micro Challenge: Offer one act of encouragement before the day ends.

Day 259: Check the Soil

Relationships
Relationships, like plants, reflect the soil they're rooted in. Neglect, distraction, or shallow care leads to withering. Consistency, attention and kindness make them grow. Strong bonds need tending before they need rescuing. The quality of your soil shapes the strength of your ties. Care for it daily.

→ **Which relationship soil could use attention?**
Micro Challenge: Send one thoughtful note or check-in to nurture a bond.

Day 260: Walk in Their Shoes

Empathy:
Empathy asks you to pause judgment and imagine standing in someone else's world. Even brief imagination softens frustration and builds compassion. People rarely need fixing as much as they need to feel seen. Empathy doesn't mean agreement; it means care. By walking in their shoes, you build trust and understanding.

→ **Who could you understand better today?**
Micro Challenge: Ask one curious question and listen without interrupting.

Day 261: Boundaries Build Safety

Boundaries:
Boundaries aren't barriers; they're safety rails. They keep relationships healthy, commitments balanced and energy steady. Without them, you slide into overwhelm and resentment. With them, you create clarity and mutual respect. Boundaries aren't rejection — they're structure. They allow you to show up at your best.

→ **Where is a missing boundary costing you peace?**
Micro Challenge: Set one clear limit today and communicate it calmly.

Day 262: Curiosity Breaks Stalemates

Curiosity:
Stalemates happen when everyone assumes they already know. Curiosity breaks the gridlock with fresh questions. Asking instead of arguing shifts energy from defence to discovery. Curiosity doesn't guarantee agreement, but it guarantees movement. Where certainty stalls, curiosity opens doors. Wonder is a strategy, not just a feeling.

→ **What question could break a stuck situation?**
Micro Challenge: Ask one new question in a place you feel stalled.

Day 263: Gratitude Anchors You

Gratitude:
Life's storms can pull you off balance. Gratitude anchors you in what's steady. Even on hard days, there are constants to name — a friend, a body that carries you, a safe place to stand. Gratitude doesn't erase pain, but it holds you firm within it. An anchored heart weathers more.

→ **What anchor of gratitude can you hold today?**
Micro Challenge: Write down three constants you're thankful for.

Day 264: Hold the Line

Grit:
Grit is the steady hand when pressure rises. It's choosing not to quit when things stretch longer or harder than expected. Many start, few finish. Holding the line when others give up is what sets you apart. Grit looks ordinary but feels extraordinary when results arrive. Stay in the fight.

→ **Where are you tempted to drop the line?**
Micro Challenge: Take one step forward in the area you've been stalling.

Day 265: Look From Above

Perspective:
Problems seem heavier when you stare only from ground level. A higher view shifts scale and gives context. Perspective reminds you that most struggles are temporary and not the whole picture. From above, challenges become chapters, not the whole story. A widened view restores calm.

→ **What would this look like from ten years ahead?**
Micro Challenge: Write one sentence describing how future-you might see it.

Day 266: Shed to Grow

Growth:
Growth isn't only about adding new habits or skills; it's also about shedding what no longer fits. Old roles, limiting beliefs and expired routines weigh you down. Releasing creates space for expansion. Nature grows by letting go first — trees drop leaves, snakes shed skins. So must you. Growth requires release.

→ **What's one thing you need to shed?**
Micro Challenge: Let go of one habit, item, or belief today.

Day 267: Reflection Strengthens Wisdom

Reflection:
Experience alone doesn't make you wiser — reflection does. Without pausing, you risk repeating the same mistakes. Reflection extracts meaning and builds patterns you can learn from. Each pause for perspective increases your strength for the next challenge. Reflection is how lessons become wisdom.

→ **What past moment still has a lesson for you?**
Micro Challenge: Journal three lines about what that moment taught you.

Day 268: Focus Creates Flow

Focus:
Flow — deep immersion in meaningful work — begins with focus. It doesn't arrive in distraction or multitasking. Choosing one challenging task and giving it full attention invites flow to appear. Focus builds the runway for creativity and energy to take off. Without it, you stay restless on the surface. Flow rewards the focused.

→ **What task deserves your flow today?**
Micro Challenge: Block 45 minutes for one task without interruption.

Day 269: Courage to Begin Again

Courage:
Starting once is hard, but beginning again after failure or pause is even harder. Pride and fear resist the restart. Courage silences them with a single new step.
Restarting proves failure isn't final. Every fresh start is a badge of resilience and strength. The brave don't just begin; they begin again.

→ **Where do you need to restart?**
Micro Challenge: Take one step today to relaunch what you left behind.

Day 270: Rise Daily

Resilience:
Resilience isn't tested only in big crises but in daily rises. Every morning is a chance to face challenges with patience and persistence. Small comebacks stack into strong resilience. Ordinary endurance builds extraordinary strength. The ability to rise daily is resilience in its purest form.

→ **How will you rise today?**
Micro Challenge: Face one challenge with patience and persistence right now.

Day 271: Discipline Builds Confidence

Discipline:
Confidence doesn't come from hype or wishes; it comes from proof. Discipline provides that proof through steady follow-through. Each kept promise builds trust in yourself. Each broken one erodes it. Confidence grows stronger every time you act with consistency. Discipline is confidence in motion.

→ **Where could discipline grow your confidence?**
Micro Challenge: Make one small promise today and keep it fully.

Day 272: Energy Requires Rest

Energy:
Energy isn't produced only by work — it's restored by rest. Without it, even your best-efforts crumble. Rest is not laziness; it's preparation for strength. When you protect rest, you protect performance and joy. A recharged mind and body create the best results. Treat rest as fuel, not reward.

→ **Where could rest restore you today?**
Micro Challenge: Take one deliberate rest break before the day ends.

Day 273: Connection Fuels Energy

Relationships:
True energy isn't only physical — it's emotional too. Relationships that uplift you act like chargers, while draining ones leave you depleted. When you choose connection with people who encourage and support you, your energy multiplies. Invest time in those who strengthen your spirit. A good conversation can be more restorative than sleep. Connection is power shared.

→ **Who lifts your energy when you're low?**
Micro Challenge: Reach out to one person today with a short message.

September Workbook – Sharpening Focus

September was about clarity — deciding what matters most and cutting out distractions. Use this page to sharpen your focus for the final quarter of the year.

1. Reflection

Where did I sharpen my focus this month?

_____
_____
_____

What distractions stole my time?

_____
_____
_____

What priorities matter most for the rest of the year?

_____
_____
_____

What tasks could I release to free my energy?

_____
_____
_____

What single focus will drive my progress in October?

_____
_____
_____

2. Journaling Prompt
Write this sentence and complete it: 'My single biggest priority for the rest of the year is…'

_____
_____
_____

3. Exercise
Draw an Eisenhower Matrix (four boxes: Urgent/Important, Not Urgent/Important, Urgent/Not Important, Not Urgent/Not Important). Sort five of your current tasks into the boxes.

[Use the space below to draw, sketch, or note your ideas.]

_____
_____
_____

October — Depth

By October, the temptation is to coast. The year has stretched long behind you and the finish line still feels far away. Energy dips and the pull toward "just getting through" is strong. But October whispers a different invitation: go deeper instead of wider. This is the month where depth becomes your strength, because depth is where real growth takes root.

Depth requires honesty. It asks you to slow down, reflect and peel back layers that daily busyness often hides. It asks you to face truths you may have avoided: What habits are only surface level? What values are truly anchoring you? Where are you pretending and where are you real? Depth is not always comfortable, but it is always transformative. The surface may look fine, but only the roots determine whether growth lasts.

Courage is necessary here. Looking inward can feel risky. It's easier to stay distracted, to keep moving quickly, to skim across the surface. But ignoring what lies beneath keeps growth shallow and fragile. October offers the chance to pause and strengthen what holds you steady. To deepen your commitment. To anchor yourself more firmly in what truly matters.

Depth does not mean doing more. It means doing less, better. It means slowing down enough to give full presence to fewer things. One conversation fully listened to. One task done with care. One practice sustained with consistency. In a culture that values speed and accumulation, depth is an act of quiet rebellion.

This month also invites deeper connections—with yourself, with others, with your purpose. Ask harder questions. Stay longer in silence. Let relationships move past small talk into honesty. Let your own journaling or reflection dig one level further than you normally allow. Growth that lasts is rarely flashy; it is rooted, steady and real.

October reminds you that surface growth fades quickly. Shallow roots dry out when the weather shifts. But deep roots endure. The habits you fortify now, the truths you face now, the values you recommit to now—these are the foundations that will carry you through the coming winter and into the next year stronger.

This is your chance to build roots. Take it.

Day 274: Curiosity Expands Possibility

Curiosity:
Curiosity takes what looks fixed and makes it flexible. Problems shrink when you ask new questions instead of repeating old answers. Every discovery begins with curiosity daring to explore. Closed minds recycle limitations; open minds generate solutions. Curiosity stretches boundaries and creates momentum where none existed. Asking is often more powerful than knowing.

→ **What new question could open a door today?**
Micro Challenge: Ask one person "What do you see that I might not?"

Day 275: Gratitude is Grounding

Gratitude:
When life moves fast, gratitude slows you down to notice the steady good. It anchors you in the present moment and reminds you not everything is chaos. Gratitude shifts your nervous system from threat to calm. Even small acknowledgments of good restore balance. It is a reset button you carry everywhere. Gratitude makes the moment liveable.

→ **What good is holding you steady today?**
Micro Challenge: Write down three things that made today easier.

Day 276: Stick Through the Middle

Grit:
Beginnings feel exciting and endings feel rewarding — but the middle is where most people quit. Grit is what keeps you moving when enthusiasm fades. The middle may feel endless, but it's where transformation actually happens. Staying there builds resilience, character and results. Push through the dull middle and breakthroughs follow. Grit holds when others drop.

→ **Where do you need to endure the middle?**
Micro Challenge: Do one extra rep, page, or minute beyond your urge to quit.

Day 277: Perspective Reduces Fear

Perspective:
Fear magnifies problems until they feel impossible. Perspective shrinks them back to scale. Looking from distance reminds you that challenges are temporary and rarely define everything. What feels permanent today is usually just a passing chapter. Perspective doesn't erase fear, but it makes it manageable. Seeing wider makes courage easier.

→ **How small will this look five years from now?**
Micro Challenge: Write one sentence reframing your fear as temporary.

Day 278: Growth Requires Feedback

Growth:
Blind spots hold back progress until someone points them out. Feedback is uncomfortable but priceless because it reveals what you can't see. Growth thrives on constructive critique, not flattery. Receiving feedback well is a super-skill of successful people. Without it, you repeat mistakes; with it, you rise stronger. Growth begins with listening.

→ **What feedback could stretch you right now?**
Micro Challenge: Ask one trusted person for one specific area to improve.

Day 279: Reflection Creates Alignment

Reflection:
It's easy to drift away from what matters in the rush of daily tasks. Reflection pulls you back to alignment with your values. Without it, success can feel hollow and aimless. With it, your actions gain clarity and purpose. Reflection is the steering wheel for the journey. Pause often to realign the direction.

→ **What choice today would bring you back into alignment with your values?**
Micro Challenge: Write down your top value and one action to honour it today.

Day 280: Focus Multiplies Momentum

Focus:
Momentum doesn't come from doing everything; it comes from repeating the right things. Focused energy compounds faster than scattered effort. Each small win adds to the next until progress accelerates. Distractions break the chain; focus strengthens it. Protect your focus to multiply momentum. It is consistency, not intensity, that wins.

→ **What deserves your undivided focus today?**
Micro Challenge: Spend 30 uninterrupted minutes on your top priority.

Day 281: Courage is Owning Mistakes

Courage:
Mistakes are inevitable, but denial magnifies them. Courage is admitting fault quickly and clearly. Owning mistakes builds trust with others and confidence in yourself. It turns failure into learning instead of shame. Apologies given with courage are seeds of stronger connection. Honesty about error is strength, not weakness.

→ **What mistake could you own today?**
Micro Challenge: Acknowledge one small mistake and name the lesson you'll carry.

Day 282: Resilience is Patience

Resilience:
Not all resilience looks like action; sometimes it looks like waiting well. Patience is the endurance of spirit that keeps you steady through delays and uncertainty. Without patience, resilience frays into panic or frustration. With patience, you preserve strength for when the breakthrough arrives. Waiting becomes less about suffering and more about preparation. Patience is power held.

→ **Where do you need more patience to be resilient?**
Micro Challenge: When impatience rises, take three slow breaths before acting.

Day 283: Discipline Shapes Identity

Discipline:
Who you are is what you repeatedly do. Each disciplined choice strengthens an identity you can trust. Over time, actions define character more than words ever could. Discipline turns values into visible habits. Skipping discipline weakens self-trust; keeping it builds unshakable belief. You become your disciplines.

→ **What identity are your current habits building?**
Micro Challenge: Name one action that reflects your best self and do it today.

Day 284: Energy Comes from Purpose

Energy:
Exhaustion often comes from doing things that don't matter. When your work connects to purpose, energy rises naturally. Purpose fuels you in ways sleep or caffeine cannot. It turns tasks into meaning and struggle into significance. Energy without purpose fades quickly. Anchor your effort in why it matters.

→ **What purpose fuels your current effort?**
Micro Challenge: Write one sentence beginning with "I'm doing this because…"

Day 285: Relationships Need Repair

Relationships:
Conflict and distance are normal in any relationship, but repair is what makes them last. Avoidance deepens cracks, while repair restores trust. A sincere apology, a hard talk, or a small act of care can heal more than silence. Strong relationships aren't free from tension; they're strong because they repair often. Repair is resilience in love.

→ **Who could you repair with today?**
Micro Challenge: Send one note or word of care to begin mending.

Day 286: Empathy Builds Bridges

Empathy:
Divides shrink when empathy grows. To pause and imagine another's perspective is to build a bridge across difference. Empathy doesn't erase disagreements but creates respect. It shifts arguments into conversations and walls into doorways. Relationships grow sturdier where empathy is practiced. Bridges hold people together.

→ Who needs a bridge of empathy from you today?
Micro Challenge: Ask one genuine question about their perspective before sharing yours.

Day 287: Boundaries Keep Balance

Boundaries:
Without boundaries, work floods into rest and obligations drown joy. Boundaries create balance by separating spaces and priorities. Saying no isn't selfish — it's structure for sanity. Boundaries protect time, energy and mental health. With them, you live balanced instead of buried. Balance is a boundary choice.

→ Where could a boundary restore balance?
Micro Challenge: Set one time block today as off-limits to outside demands.

Day 288: Curiosity Sparks Connection

Curiosity:
People open up when they feel someone is truly interested. Curiosity deepens conversations and makes others feel valued. Instead of assuming, curiosity asks and listens. Connection grows stronger through genuine questions. Wonder isn't just for learning — it's for loving too. Curiosity turns strangers into allies.

→ **Who could you get curious about today?**
Micro Challenge: Ask one person a question you've never asked them before.

Day 289: Gratitude Reframes the Day

Gratitude:
Days aren't defined only by what went wrong — gratitude rewrites the script. Focusing on what went right softens stress and highlights joy. Even small moments, like a smile or a meal, shift perspective. Gratitude reminds you that good exists alongside struggle. The day feels different when you count the gifts. Gratitude is a lens you can choose.

→ **What bright spot can you name from today?**
Micro Challenge: Write down three positive moments before bed.

Day 290: Stay the Course

Grit:
Momentum builds slowly, but grit stays steady when results lag. It's easy to quit when progress feels invisible. Grit holds faith that consistency compounds. Small steps add up even if no one notices today. Over time, grit outpaces talent and luck. Stay the course — your persistence is the secret.

→ **Where are you tempted to stop too soon?**
Micro Challenge: Take one small step forward in that area today.

Day 291: Perspective Brings Calm

Perspective:
Stress rises when problems fill your whole view. Perspective reminds you they're only part of the picture. Stepping back shrinks intensity and opens options. The story you tell yourself about the challenge shapes how you feel. From a wider lens, pressure eases. Perspective is peace regained.

→ **What would a calmer angle show you?**
Micro Challenge: Rewrite today's biggest stressor in one balanced sentence.

Day 292: Growth Loves Challenge

Growth:
Comfort feels safe but suffocates progress. Growth thrives in challenge because it stretches your skills and mindset. Every obstacle is a training ground for expansion. Resistance builds strength only if you face it. Growth rarely feels easy, but it always feels worthwhile in hindsight. Choose the challenge and let it shape you.

→ **What challenge could grow you right now?**
Micro Challenge: Do one task today that feels slightly beyond your comfort zone.

Day 293: Reflection Brings Clarity

Reflection:
Busyness can blur your direction until everything feels urgent. Reflection cuts through the blur by asking what actually matters. A few quiet minutes can save hours of wasted effort. Reflection turns noise into signal and confusion into clarity. Without it, you chase everything; with it, you chase the right things. Clarity is born in pause.

→ **What's one thing worth keeping and one thing worth cutting?**
Micro Challenge: Spend five minutes listing your top three priorities today.

Day 294: Focus Creates Simplicity

Focus:
Life feels overwhelming when everything matters equally. Focus simplifies by choosing what matters most and letting the rest wait. Simplicity is the fruit of disciplined attention. The more you focus, the lighter life becomes. Doing less with depth beats doing more with distraction. Simplicity is power refined.

→ **What one thing would simplify your day if done first?**
Micro Challenge: Identify and finish that one thing before noon.

Day 295: Courage Faces the Mirror

Courage:
It takes courage to face yourself honestly. Seeing your flaws without denial or defensiveness is the first step toward change. Self-honesty can sting, but it heals faster than self-deception. The mirror may reveal weakness, but it also reveals opportunity. Courage in self-reflection creates growth others can see. Bravery begins with truth to yourself.

→ **What truth about yourself are you avoiding?**
Micro Challenge: Write down one habit you need to change and one step to start.

Day 296: Resilience Learns Flexibility

Resilience:
Stubbornness resists change, but resilience adapts. Flexibility keeps you moving when conditions shift. The goal can stay the same, but the path can change. Adaptation is not weakness — it's survival. Resilience grows when you allow yourself to pivot. Strength bends and endures.

→ **Where do you need to adapt instead of resist?**
Micro Challenge: Change one small approach to make progress today.

Day 297: Discipline Keeps Promises

Discipline:
Trust in yourself grows when you do what you said you'd do. Each kept promise, no matter how small, strengthens your self-belief. Breaking promises erodes that trust quietly but quickly. Discipline is how you prove your words true through action. Over time, kept promises create confidence and integrity. Promise-keeping is self-respect.

→ **What promise do you need to keep today?**
Micro Challenge: Choose one small promise and follow through before bed.

Day 298: Energy Needs Rhythm

Energy:
Constant pushing drains energy, but rhythm restores it. Life has seasons of work, play and rest — ignoring them creates burnout. Matching your effort to natural rhythms creates endurance. Energy thrives when it cycles, not when it's squeezed. Rest and action together make you strong. Rhythm is wisdom at work.

→ **Where do you need to reset your rhythm?**
Micro Challenge: Pause once today to rest deliberately before resuming.

Day 299: Relationships Need Presence

Relationships:
Presence is the rarest gift in distracted times. Being fully with someone — no phone, no split attention — communicates value deeper than words. Relationships weaken when presence is missing and strengthen when it's practiced. Even short moments of full attention can transform connection. Presence is proof of love.

→ **Who deserves your full attention today?**
Micro Challenge: In your next conversation, put the phone away and truly listen.

Day 300: Empathy Softens Conflict

Empathy:
Conflict hardens when both sides cling only to their view. Empathy softens it by imagining the other's perspective. It doesn't mean you agree, but it means you respect. Understanding creates room for resolution where force cannot. Empathy turns confrontation into collaboration. Listening is often the loudest solution.

→ **Where could empathy ease tension today?**
Micro Challenge: Repeat back what the other person said before giving your view.

Day 301: Boundaries Protect Peace

Boundaries:
Your peace of mind is fragile if you don't protect it. Without boundaries, stress and noise invade every corner of your life. With them, calm has space to grow. Peace is not accidental — it's defended. Boundaries are your shield against chaos. Protecting peace protects everything else.

→ **What boundary could restore peace right now?**
Micro Challenge: Turn off one channel of noise for the rest of the day.

Day 302: Curiosity Creates Joy

Curiosity:
Curiosity isn't just for solving problems — it creates joy. Seeing life with fresh eyes makes ordinary moments sparkle. Asking "What's here I haven't noticed?" makes the world feel alive again. Wonder keeps the heart young. Curiosity adds delight to daily life.

→ **Where could curiosity brighten today?**
Micro Challenge: Try one new thing you've never done before.

Day 303: Gratitude Expands Enough

Gratitude:
Scarcity whispers, "Not enough." Gratitude answers, "More than enough." When you count what you have, your world grows larger. Comparison shrinks joy, but gratitude expands it. Enough isn't a number — it's a perspective. Gratitude shifts lack into abundance.

→ **What do you already have more than enough of?**
Micro Challenge: Write down three areas where your needs are already met.

Day 304: Grit Outlasts Excuses

Grit:
Excuses appear when effort feels heavy. Grit outlasts them by acting anyway. Excuses fade when consistency builds results. Grit is choosing discipline over distraction and progress over procrastination. It doesn't require perfection, only persistence. Outlasting excuses turns obstacles into victories.

→ **What excuse do you need to silence today?**
Micro Challenge: Do one action you've been postponing — no delay.

October Workbook – Going Deeper

October invited you to stop skimming the surface and go deeper into your values, commitments and habits. Growth comes from depth, not speed. Use this page to reflect on what deepened this month.

1. Reflection

Where did I deepen my commitment this month?

_____
_____
_____

What truth about myself did I face?

_____
_____
_____

What values felt strongest?

_____
_____
_____

What routines or habits became more meaningful?

_____
_____
_____

What am I ready to deepen further in November?

_____

_____

2. Journaling Prompt

Journal on this: 'What area of my life deserves more honesty and attention?'

_____

_____

3. Exercise

Draw a tree. In the roots, write your values. In the trunk, your habits. In the branches, your outcomes. Notice how deep roots support strong branches.

[Use the space below to draw, sketch, or note your ideas.]

_____

_____

November — Gratitude

November is the season of gratitude. As the year begins to draw toward its close, this month invites you to pause, notice and give thanks. After months of striving, building, stretching and enduring, gratitude brings balance. It is the moment to take a breath and to recognise what has been gained—not only in outcomes, but in lessons, resilience and presence.

Gratitude changes perspective. It shifts focus from what's missing to what's already here. Without it, the year can feel like a blur of effort, a long stretch of unfinished goals and unmet expectations. With gratitude, the same year looks different—you see richness, progress and quiet blessings that may have gone unnoticed. Gratitude grounds you in what matters most.

This month, let gratitude become a practice, not just a passing thought. Write it down. Speak it out loud. Share it with others. Keep a running list or simply pause each evening to name three things you're thankful for. Gratitude multiplies joy. It strengthens relationships. It even makes endurance lighter, because it shifts the weight from what you lack to what you've been given.

Gratitude is not denial of hardship. It doesn't erase the struggle or pretend everything is easy. Instead, it sits beside difficulty and reminds you that struggle and blessing often coexist. The setbacks taught lessons. The challenges built strength. The moments of joy, no matter how small, became anchors in the storm. Gratitude helps you hold both truths at once.

November is also about balance. It asks you to finish the year strong, but not only through relentless pursuit of progress. Strength is found just as much in remembering what you already have. By acknowledging the good— the support, the opportunities, the lessons, even the resilience you've discovered—you refuel yourself for the final stretch. Gratitude makes the heavy feel lighter. It makes the ordinary shine brighter.

So let November be your reminder: pause long enough to notice. Write the thank-you note. Say the words out loud. Look around with softer eyes. Gratitude is not just a feeling; it is a practice that turns what you have into enough and enough into abundance.

The season may be darker, the days shorter, but gratitude makes everything brighter.

Day 305: Perspective Lifts the Weight

Perspective:
The same problem feels heavier or lighter depending on how you frame it. Seeing it as punishment drains you; seeing it as training strengthens you. Perspective doesn't erase the struggle, but it changes how you carry it. A wider lens brings balance, calm and strength. You decide the story your challenge tells.

→ **How could you reframe today's load?**
Micro Challenge: Write one sentence that casts your challenge as training.

Day 306: Growth Needs Stretch

Growth:
You cannot grow while staying fully comfortable. Stretch is the signal that capacity is expanding. Muscles strengthen under tension and so do minds. Each stretch feels unnatural at first but later becomes your new normal. Growth demands edges, not easy spaces. Lean into the stretch to rise.

→ **What small stretch could expand you today?**
Micro Challenge: Do one task just outside your comfort zone.

Day 307: Reflection Builds Self-Awareness

Reflection:
Without reflection, you may repeat mistakes without noticing. Pausing helps you see patterns, lessons and progress. Self-awareness grows when you give yourself time to examine choices. Reflection turns life into a classroom instead of a blur. What you review, you can improve. Awareness is strength in disguise.

→ **What moment deserves reflection today?**
Micro Challenge: Write three lines about what you learned this week.

Day 308: Focus Turns Effort into Results

Focus:
Effort alone doesn't guarantee outcomes — focus does. When you spread yourself thin, you create activity, not progress. Directing full attention at one meaningful task transforms effort into results. Focus makes the difference between being busy and being effective. Your results reveal what you've focused on most.

→ **What result needs your focus right now?**
Micro Challenge: Work for 30 minutes on one task without distraction.

Day 309: Courage is Choosing Vulnerability

Courage:
Vulnerability feels risky, but it builds connection and trust. Admitting weakness, asking for help, or sharing feelings requires bravery. Courage isn't always loud; sometimes it's quiet honesty. Vulnerability clears walls and invites real support. The strongest bonds are built on courageous openness.

→ **Where could vulnerability serve you today?**
Micro Challenge: Share one truth you normally keep guarded.

Day 310: Resilience Thrives on Perspective

Resilience:
Resilience grows when you see setbacks as part of the bigger story. One failure doesn't erase your path forward. Perspective transforms obstacles into temporary bumps, not permanent blocks. Every comeback proves your capacity to endure. Resilience is strengthened by seeing beyond the moment. Step back and strength grows.

→ **What setback could be reframed as temporary?**
Micro Challenge: Name one lesson your setback has already taught.

Day 311: Discipline Brings Stability

Discipline:
Life feels chaotic when discipline is absent. Consistent habits create stability, even in uncertain times. Structure frees you from relying on mood or motivation. Discipline is the anchor that steadies progress. Without it, you drift; with it, you direct. Stability is built through steady action.

→ **What habit could steady you today?**
Micro Challenge: Do one small action at the same time you did yesterday.

Day 312: Energy Demands Boundaries

Energy:
You can't pour endlessly without refilling. Boundaries keep your energy from leaking into everything. Protecting your capacity isn't selfish — it's survival. When you choose where to invest, you preserve strength for what matters. Guarded energy fuels sharper work and kinder presence. Protect the tank.

→ **Where do you need to draw an energy line?**
Micro Challenge: Say no to one drain and yes to one rest today.

Day 313: Relationships Are Built in Listening

Relationships:
Listening is one of the simplest yet rarest gifts you can give. People feel valued when they are heard without interruption or judgment. Listening builds trust more than any speech ever could. Relationships thrive when space is made for another's voice. To listen well is to love well.

→ **Who needs your listening today?**
Micro Challenge: Ask one person how they're doing and truly listen.

Day 314: Empathy Strengthens Leadership

Empathy:
Leaders without empathy command obedience, but leaders with empathy earn commitment. Empathy connects vision to people and authority to trust. It humanises leadership by showing care alongside direction. People don't forget how you made them feel. Empathy turns management into inspiration.

→ **Where could empathy make you a stronger leader?**
Micro Challenge: Ask one person what support they need today.

Day 315: Boundaries Keep You Whole

Boundaries:
Saying yes to everything pulls you apart. Boundaries keep you whole by protecting time, values and peace. Without them, resentment grows; with them, clarity strengthens. Boundaries aren't rejection but redirection toward what matters most. Keeping yourself whole helps you give more authentically.

→ **Where are you saying yes at your own expense?**
Micro Challenge: Choose one small no that preserves your peace.

Day 316: Curiosity Walls into Doors

Curiosity:
When you hit a wall, curiosity asks where the door might be. Assumptions freeze progress, but questions create movement. Curiosity shifts you from stuck to searching. Exploration reveals options you hadn't considered. The problem may not shrink, but your possibilities will expand. Curiosity keeps progress alive.

→ **What question could open a door today?**
Micro Challenge: Ask one new "what if" about your challenge.

Day 317: Gratitude Strengthens Resilience

Gratitude:
Gratitude doesn't remove hardship, but it fuels the endurance to face it. Naming what's steady keeps you from collapsing under what's unstable. Gratitude balances despair with hope. The more you notice, the stronger you stand. Resilience grows when gratitude steadies the ground beneath you. Gratitude is survival fuel.

→ **What steady good can you name right now?**
Micro Challenge. Write three things you're grateful for, despite difficulty.

Day 318: Grit Holds Through Silence

Grit:
Progress isn't always loud or obvious. Sometimes grit looks like showing up quietly, even when no one notices. Sticking to the plan in silence builds inner strength. Grit doesn't crave applause; it craves progress. Endurance in unseen moments is where grit is forged.

→ **Where are you building quietly?**
Micro Challenge: Do one action today without telling anyone.

Day 319: Perspective Brings Balance

Perspective:
Without perspective, one problem can feel like your whole life. Stepping back reminds you of the many other good things still standing. Perspective rebalances attention so no single issue defines you. Challenges shrink when you see them in proportion. Balance is born from broader vision.

→ **What else is true alongside this problem?**
Micro Challenge: Write down three areas of life that are still stable.

Day 320: Growth Demands Change

Growth:
You cannot grow without changing. Staying the same feels safe, but it stalls progress. Change stretch's identity, skill and confidence. Each shift, even small, is proof of expansion. Growth doesn't wait for perfect timing — it begins with change today.

→ **What change could fuel your growth?**
Micro Challenge: Start one new habit or release one old one today.

Day 321: Reflection Reveals Progress

Reflection:
Progress often hides in the day-to-day grind. Reflection makes it visible by showing how far you've come. Looking back proves that consistency works. Without reflection, you may underestimate your growth. With it, you encourage yourself to keep going. Reflection is progress revealed.

→ **Where have you grown that you haven't noticed?**
Micro Challenge: List three ways you've improved in the last 6 months.

Day 322: Focus Directs Power

Focus:
Energy without focus scatters like sunlight through clouds. Focus directs it into power, like a laser. Choosing one priority channels effort into real change. Without focus, activity multiplies but results vanish. With focus, your power is magnified. Direction determines impact.

→ **What deserves your power today?**
Micro Challenge: Choose one task and give it undivided attention.

Day 323: Courage to Stand Alone

Courage:
Sometimes courage means standing for what's right even if no one stands with you. Popularity may fade, but integrity remains. Choosing your values over approval is bravery in its truest form. Standing alone today builds strength for tomorrow. Courage isn't measured by crowd size but by conviction.

→ **Where do you need to stand alone?**
Micro Challenge: Say one no or one truth, even if no one joins you.

Day 324: Resilience Rebuilds Trust

Resilience:
Broken trust can feel final, but resilience gives it a chance to rebuild. Trust isn't restored overnight — it grows through consistent actions over time. Showing up repeatedly with honesty and integrity strengthens bonds again. Resilience is the patience to repair slowly. Relationships can heal when resilience fuels them.

→ **Where could resilience repair trust for you?**
Micro Challenge: Do one small action today that rebuilds trust.

Day 325: Discipline Protects Integrity

Discipline:
Integrity isn't only about big choices — it's about daily consistency. Doing what you said, even when no one watches, builds character. Discipline is how you guard that consistency. Without it, integrity slips; with it, your actions align with your words. Integrity is discipline proven daily.

→ **What daily action proves your integrity?**
Micro Challenge: Keep one small promise to yourself today.

Day 326: Energy Flows from Renewal

Energy:
Effort drains, but renewal restores. Without regular renewal, you burn out. Renewal can be rest, creativity, nature, or play. Energy flows when you balance work with recovery. You can't pour endlessly without filling back up. Renewal is essential fuel.

→ **What renewal practice restores you most?**
Micro Challenge: Spend 15 minutes today doing something that restores you.

Day 327: Relationships Need Consistency

Relationships:
Consistency builds stronger bonds than occasional grand gestures. Small, steady signals of care matter more than once-in-a-while intensity. People trust what you repeat. Relationships grow when consistency shows you mean it. A steady presence builds lasting ties.

→ **Who could use your consistent care today?**
Micro Challenge: Send one small check-in to someone you value.

Day 328: Empathy Heals Division

Empathy:
Division thrives on assumptions and judgments. Empathy interrupts it by seeking to understand. Listening with care softens anger and creates space for resolution. Empathy doesn't erase differences, but it heals the divide between people. Understanding is often the first step to peace.

→ **Where could empathy heal a divide today?**
Micro Challenge: Listen to someone you disagree with without interrupting.

Day 329: Boundaries Guard Your Future

Boundaries:
Every commitment today shapes your tomorrow. Boundaries protect your future from being consumed by short-term demands. Saying no now creates space for long-term yes. Without boundaries, tomorrow gets sacrificed to today's noise. Guard your future with present discipline.

→ **What boundary could protect your tomorrow?**
Micro Challenge: Say no to one thing that doesn't serve your future self.

Day 330: Curiosity Fuels Learning

Curiosity:
Learning doesn't stop with school — it thrives on curiosity. Asking "why" and "how" keeps your mind alive and growing. Curiosity feeds innovation and adaptability. Without it, you stagnate; with it, you evolve. Growth is fuelled by the questions you dare to ask.

→ **What do you want to learn today?**
Micro Challenge: Ask one question that stretches your understanding.

Day 331: Gratitude Strengthens Relationships

Gratitude:
Unspoken appreciation weakens bonds over time. Gratitude expressed keeps relationships alive and strong. People thrive when they feel noticed and valued. Saying thank you often is simple but powerful. Gratitude is the glue that strengthens connection.

→ **Who deserves your thanks today?**
Micro Challenge: Tell one person specifically why you appreciate them.

Day 332: Grit Chooses Consistency

Grit:
Talent shines briefly, but grit stays steady. Grit is showing up again and again, especially when progress feels invisible. Consistency compounds into strength others can't see coming. The quiet choice to persist outlasts bursts of effort. Grit is the art of consistency over time.

→ **Where do you need consistency most?**
Micro Challenge: Do one small action for the same goal today.

Day 333: Perspective Restores Hope

Perspective:
Hopelessness grows when problems dominate your view. Perspective restores hope by reminding you of the bigger picture. Most struggles are temporary and not the whole story. Seeing beyond the present difficulty brings calm. Perspective is a doorway back to hope.

→ **What hope can perspective restore for you?**
Micro Challenge: Write one sentence about how this will pass.

Day 334: Growth Loves Discomfort

Growth:
Discomfort is not failure — it's evidence of growth. Every stretch feels awkward before it feels natural. Without discomfort, you remain unchanged. Growth comes by stepping into what feels uneasy. Discomfort today is strength tomorrow. Embrace it as a sign of progress.

→ **Where could discomfort mean growth for you?**
Micro Challenge: Choose one small action that feels slightly uncomfortable.

November Workbook – Gratitude Practice

November was a month to practice gratitude — to see blessings in the ordinary, to count the small wins and to say thank you more often. Use this page to anchor that gratitude in writing.

1. Reflection

What am I most thankful for this month?

_____
_____
_____

Where did gratitude shift my perspective?

_____
_____
_____

Who supported me that I haven't yet thanked?

_____
_____
_____

What daily blessings do I want to notice more often?

_____
_____
_____

How can I carry gratitude into December?

_____
_____
_____

2. Journaling Prompt
Write a gratitude letter to someone important (you don't have to send it). Capture your feelings honestly.

_____
_____
_____

3. Exercise
Make a Gratitude Web: write your name in the centre and draw lines outward to people, events, or habits you're grateful for. Add as many as possible.

[Use the space below to draw, sketch, or note your ideas.]

_____
_____
_____

December — Legacy

December is the year's closing chapter. The final page before a new one begins. It is not just about endings; it is about legacy. What have your choices added up to? What story has this year told? Every day you showed up, every moment of pause, every stumble and restart has been part of that story. Now is the time to step back and see the whole arc.

Legacy is not built in grand gestures. It is built in daily repetition. The small, steady acts of courage, the quiet discipline when no one was watching, the moments of gratitude whispered in passing—these are what create lasting impact. December is the month to notice the thread that runs through it all. Look back and see how each reflection, each challenge, each act of persistence became part of something larger.

This month invites you to reflect deeply. Celebrate progress, however imperfect. Acknowledge the missteps without shame—because they, too, shaped your resilience. Gather the lessons you want to carry forward. Legacy is not about flawless achievement; it is about consistency, about proving to yourself that you can keep moving even when the path felt unclear.

December also asks you to honour the journey. Too often, we rush into January, eager for a clean slate, without pausing to truly appreciate the year we've just lived. Slow down. Reflect. Give thanks for what was gained, for what was endured and even for what was lost—because all of it has been part of your becoming.

This is also the season for closing circles. Finish what can be finished. Release what cannot. Offer forgiveness where it's needed, both to yourself and to others.

Clearing space now ensures that you step into the new year unburdened, carrying forward only what matters.

Legacy is built one day at a time. And this year, day by day, you've proven that growth is possible. You've endured resistance, renewed commitment, built momentum, stretched courage, strengthened resilience and cultivated gratitude. You are stronger than yesterday—not just in skill, but in spirit. That is a legacy worth celebrating.

So let December be both closure and blessing. Honour the journey behind you. Prepare with hope for the one ahead. The story of this year is complete—and it has made you ready for the next.

Day 335: Reflection Guides Tomorrow

Reflection:
Reflection isn't just about the past — it guides the future. Looking back clarifies what to repeat and what to avoid. Reflection helps you refine your choices moving forward. The past becomes fuel for better tomorrows. Without reflection, mistakes recycle; with it, growth accelerates.

→ **What lesson should guide tomorrow?**
Micro Challenge: Write down one past insight and apply it today.

Day 336: Focus Creates Mastery

Focus:
Mastery isn't born from dabbling but from deep focus. When you give one skill or pursuit consistent attention, it sharpens and grows. Spreading thin creates mediocrity; narrowing deepens excellence. Focus is the path from average to exceptional. What you repeat with attention becomes what you master.

→ **What deserves deep focus for mastery?**
Micro Challenge: Spend one hour today improving a single skill.

Day 337: Courage is Quiet Persistence

Courage:
Courage doesn't always roar; sometimes it's a whisper to keep going. Showing up consistently when no one notices takes bravery. Quiet persistence builds strength more than dramatic moments do. Each small act of courage lays a foundation of resilience. Bravery grows in steady steps.

→ **Where could quiet courage carry you today?**
Micro Challenge: Take one action today that no one else will see.

Day 338: Resilience is Choosing Again

Resilience:
Resilience is the power to choose again after disappointment. Failure tempts you to stop, but resilience reminds you to decide once more. Each new choice is proof that setbacks don't define you. Choosing again builds confidence that you can rise, no matter what. Strength is in the repeated decision.

→ **What could you choose again today?**
Micro Challenge: Recommit to one dropped goal with a single small step.

Day 339: Discipline Turns Chaos into Order

Discipline:
Without discipline, days spiral into distraction and regret. With it, order replaces chaos and intention replaces impulse. Discipline isn't rigid control but consistent structure. Small disciplines ripple into clarity across your life. The habits you protect shape the person you become. Order grows from repeated choices.

→ **What discipline could bring order to your day?**
Micro Challenge: Keep one daily routine no matter what.

Day 340: Energy Flows Where Attention Goes

Energy:
Energy follows focus. When you dwell on problems, you feel drained; when you focus on purpose, you feel fuelled. Your attention is a switch that directs energy. Guard it wisely, because it decides how you feel. Direct attention creates directed energy.

→ **Where is your attention fuelling or draining you?**
Micro Challenge: Redirect focus from a worry to one purposeful action.

Day 341: Relationships Grow with Honesty

Relationships:
Honesty is the oxygen that keeps relationships alive. Without it, connections suffocate under pretence. Truth builds trust, even when it stings. Honest words spoken with care deepen respect and intimacy. Real relationships require real words.

→ **Who needs honesty from you today?**
Micro Challenge: Speak one truth kindly but clearly to someone close.

Day 342: Empathy Creates Safety

Empathy:
Safety in relationships grows when people feel understood. Empathy creates that safety by listening and caring without judgment. It doesn't demand fixing — only presence. When empathy is present, walls fall and openness rises. Safety is the soil where trust grows.

→ **Who needs to feel safe with you today?**
Micro Challenge: Listen fully without offering advice.

Day 343: Boundaries Guard Mental Health

Boundaries:
Your mind needs fences just like your time does. Without boundaries, stress and noise invade until you feel overwhelmed. Boundaries protect peace, focus and stability. Guarding your mental space is an act of strength, not weakness. Clear lines protect clear minds.

→ **What mental boundary could protect you today?**
Micro Challenge: Turn off one source of negative input for 24 hours.

Day 344: Curiosity Fuels Innovation

Curiosity:
Innovation rarely comes from knowing — it comes from wondering. Curiosity questions assumptions and imagines new possibilities. Every breakthrough began with someone asking, "What if?" Closed minds recycle the same results. Open minds invent better ones. Curiosity is the seed of change.

→ **What assumption could you question today?**
Micro Challenge: Ask "What if this could be done differently?" about one task.

Day 345: Gratitude Expands Joy

Gratitude:
Joy multiplies when gratitude is practiced daily. Small thanks turn ordinary moments into treasures. Gratitude doesn't need perfect conditions — it finds light even in shadows. The more you notice, the more joy grows. Appreciation is joy's doorway.

→ **What small joy can you thank today?**
Micro Challenge: Write down three moments of joy before bed.

Day 346: Grit Stays When Others Leave

Grit:
Many people quit when the path gets rough. Grit is what keeps you walking. It's not flashy but steady, the quiet decision to outlast. Grit doesn't guarantee quick results, but it guarantees progress. Staying power is strength disguised as stubbornness.

→ **Where do you need to outlast today?**
Micro Challenge: Take one step further where you feel like stopping.

Day 347: Perspective Creates Options

Perspective:
When problems fill your entire view, options seem invisible. A shift in perspective reveals choices you couldn't see. Stepping back creates room for creativity and calm. Often the problem isn't the problem — it's the angle. Change the angle and new doors appear.

→ **What other angle could you view this from?**
Micro Challenge: Write one alternative explanation for your challenge.

Day 348: Growth is Daily Practice

Growth:
Growth doesn't happen in leaps but in repeated practice. Small efforts layered over time expand skill and confidence. Every day is a chance to stretch a little more. Missed days don't erase progress; returning to practice keeps it alive. Growth is the product of persistence, not perfection.

→ **What practice could you return to today?**
Micro Challenge: Repeat one growth habit you've skipped lately.

Day 349: Reflection Creates Meaning

Reflection:
Life without reflection feels like noise without melody. Pausing to reflect creates meaning from the chaos. It allows you to connect dots, learn lessons and notice progress. Reflection doesn't change events, but it changes your experience of them. Meaning grows when reflection gives context.

→ **What meaning can reflection reveal today?**
Micro Challenge: Spend five minutes journaling about one lesson from this week.

Day 350: Focus Builds Strength

Focus:
Strength doesn't come from doing everything — it comes from doing the right thing with focus. Concentrated effort builds endurance and mastery. Distractions scatter strength until nothing sticks. Focused attention creates momentum and resilience. Every moment of focus makes you stronger.

→ **Where could focus strengthen you today?**
Micro Challenge: Set a timer and give full focus to one task.

Day 351: Courage Confronts Fear

Courage:
Fear whispers reasons to wait, but courage moves anyway. Courage isn't the absence of fear but the refusal to obey it. Facing what scares you builds confidence and freedom. Fear shrinks when confronted but grows when avoided. Bravery begins with one step forward.

→ **What fear needs confronting today?**
Micro Challenge: Do one action you've delayed out of fear.

Day 352: Resilience Holds Hope

Resilience:
Resilience doesn't deny pain — it holds hope inside it. Hope gives you strength to endure and rebuild. Even in hardship, resilience whispers, "This is not the end." With hope, you can rise again and again. Hope is resilience's secret ally.

→ **What hope could strengthen you now?**
Micro Challenge: Write down one reason tomorrow could be better.

Day 353: Discipline Creates Confidence

Discipline:
Confidence isn't born from words — it's built from evidence. Every disciplined act proves you can rely on yourself. Self-trust grows when your actions match your promises. Confidence grows step by step through daily discipline. The more you keep showing up, the stronger you believe.

→ **What disciplined act could build confidence today?**
Micro Challenge: Keep one promise you've been tempted to skip.

Day 354: Energy is Created, Not Just Spent

Energy:
Energy doesn't only drain — it also generates. Movement, purpose and connection fuel energy more than rest alone. What you do can lift you higher instead of wearing you down. Don't just protect energy — create it. Energy grows when you engage fully.

→ **What activity could create energy for you today?**
Micro Challenge: Do one action that recharges instead of drains.

Day 355: Relationships Thrive on Appreciation

Relationships:
Appreciation is fuel for connection. Relationships weaken when gratitude is unspoken but thrive when thanks are expressed. Small acknowledgments carry more weight than you realise. Appreciation turns ordinary bonds into lasting ones. The more you give, the stronger they grow.

→ **Who deserves your appreciation today?**
Micro Challenge: Express thanks to one person before the day ends.

Day 356: Empathy Eases Tension

Empathy:
Tension escalates when no one feels understood. Empathy defuses it by showing you care enough to listen. A simple acknowledgment of feelings can calm conflict. People soften when they feel seen. Empathy often resolves what arguments cannot.

→ **Where could empathy ease tension for you today?**
Micro Challenge: Reflect back what you heard before sharing your own view.

Day 357: Boundaries Protect Focus

Boundaries:
Every distraction steals from your priority. Boundaries are fences that keep your focus intact. Protecting your time means defending your future. Without boundaries, you live scattered; with them, you live sharp. Focus requires defence.

→ **What boundary could protect your focus today?**
Micro Challenge: Turn off notifications for one focused work block.

Day 358: Curiosity Keeps Life Fresh

Curiosity:
Routine can dull your days, but curiosity revives them. A fresh question or new experience brings energy back. Curiosity turns boredom into discovery. It's how you keep growing and stay alive to the world. Wonder is a choice that refreshes.

→ **Where could curiosity refresh you today?**
Micro Challenge: Try one small new experience before the day ends.

Day 359: Gratitude Replaces Comparison

Gratitude:
Comparison steals joy by focusing on others' lives. Gratitude replaces it by focusing on your own. When you notice what you already have, envy fades. Gratitude reminds you your life is already rich. Enough lives where gratitude looks.

→ **What could gratitude help you stop comparing?**
Micro Challenge: List three things you wouldn't trade for anyone else's.

Day 360: Grit Stays the Course

Grit:
The hardest part of any journey is staying when progress slows. Grit is the strength to keep walking anyway. It outlasts fatigue, boredom and discouragement. Grit turns small steps into big gains over time. Staying the course is victory in motion.

→ **Where do you need to keep going?**
Micro Challenge: Do one small step in the place you feel stuck.

Day 361: Perspective Reveals Blessings

Perspective:
A shift in perspective can turn a burden into a blessing. Often what feels heavy today becomes the reason for tomorrow's strength. Perspective allows you to see the gift within the grind. Your view shapes your experience more than the circumstance does. Blessings are often hidden until perspective changes.

→ **What hidden blessing could this challenge hold?**
Micro Challenge: Write one benefit that might come from your struggle.

Day 362: Growth Requires Courage

Growth:
Growth and courage are always linked. To grow, you must risk failure, embarrassment, or uncertainty. Courage stretches you into spaces you haven't mastered yet. Without courage, growth stalls in safety. Every bold step expands your capacity. Courage is growth in motion.

→ **What risk could grow you today?**
Micro Challenge: Take one bold step into discomfort.

Day 363: Reflection Brings Peace

Reflection:
Peace doesn't come only from escape — it comes from understanding. Reflection helps you make sense of what happened so you can carry it lighter. When you see meaning in experience, the weight softens. Reflection turns chaos into clarity and rest. Pausing to reflect restores peace within.

→ **What reflection could bring you peace today?**
Micro Challenge: Write three lines about what you've learned this month.

Day 364: Focus Finishes Strong

Focus:
Beginnings are easy; endings require focus. The temptation near the finish line is to coast, but focus helps you finish strong. Concentrated effort at the end creates lasting impact. Focus ensures you close well, not just start well. How you finish shapes how you're remembered.

→ **Where do you need focus to finish strong?**
Micro Challenge: Identify your top unfinished task and complete it.

Day 365: Live the Legacy

Discipline:
Your legacy is built in daily actions, not distant dreams. Discipline is how you live the story you want to leave. Each choice shapes the mark you make. Living aligned with values every day creates a legacy without effort. Your future is written in today's discipline. Begin now, not later.

→ **What legacy are you living today?**
Micro Challenge: Choose one value and act on it before the day ends.

December Workbook – Legacy Ledger

December asks you to look back at the year as a whole — the story you wrote through your habits, choices and mindset. Use this page to define your legacy for the year and what you want to carry forward.

1. Reflection

What story did this year tell?

_____
_____
_____

What daily habits shaped me most?

_____
_____
_____

What am I most proud of sustaining?

_____
_____
_____

What do I want to release as the year closes?

_____
_____
_____

What do I want to carry into the new year?

_____
_____
_____

2. Journaling Prompt
Write a message to your future self-one year from now. What do you want to remind them of?

_____
_____
_____

3. Exercise
Create a 'Legacy Ledger.' Two columns: 'Habits to Keep' and 'Habits to Release.' Fill them honestly. Sign and date it as your personal contract for the future.

[Use the space below to draw, sketch, or note your ideas.]

_____
_____
_____

Outro – Stronger Than Yesterday

A year is complete. Three hundred and sixty-five days of reflection, questions and action. You began with curiosity and commitment. You stayed steady when it was hard. You renewed, endured, focused and deepened. You practiced gratitude, showed courage and built resilience. Day by day, you became stronger than yesterday.

And now here you are, standing at the close of one chapter and the beginning of another.

But this is not the end. Growth doesn't stop because the calendar resets. Progress is not bound by months, nor do lessons vanish when the year turns over. What you've practiced here—reflection, consistency, discipline, courage—these are not temporary experiments. They are lifelong tools, forged and tested, ready to carry forward into whatever comes next.

Think about what has happened over these twelve months. January offered the clean slate, the gentle beginning. You learned that consistency mattered more than perfection. February taught you steadiness, the art of showing up even when the novelty had worn off. March called you to renewal, to recommit when the shine faded. April gave you momentum, that rolling force that carried you further than you once thought possible. May tested endurance, where grit replaced glamour and the grind became your teacher.

Then came June, the mirror month, asking you to reflect honestly on what had been built. July invited boldness, courage to step forward even in fear. August pressed resilience into your bones, teaching you to rise, recover and begin again. September sharpened your clarity, cutting distractions so focus could thrive. October pulled you deeper, teaching that true growth requires roots, not just surface change. November wrapped your work in gratitude, reminding you of the strength found in joy and appreciation. And December closed the circle, weaving your efforts into legacy—proof that you are not the same as when you began.

This has not been a random journey. Each month built on the last. Each theme carried you forward, layering discipline over reflection, courage over endurance, gratitude over grit. What you hold now is not a scattered collection of practices but a woven fabric of resilience and growth.

Looking Ahead

So, what comes next? Another year. Another cycle. Another 365 opportunities. But more than that, another chance to live out what you've learned.

Here's the truth: the tools you built this year are not meant to be stored away. They are meant to be lived. Reflection, consistency, courage, resilience, gratitude, depth, clarity—these are not seasonal decorations but daily companions. Carry them with you. Let them shape how you meet the unknown.

The year ahead will bring its own challenges. You may meet unexpected opportunities. You may face setbacks you did not plan for. You may also achieve victories you once thought out of reach. Whatever arrives, the same truth applies you are ready. Not because you will never struggle, but because you know how to continue.

The temptation will be to sprint into the new year with a dozen resolutions and promises. Resist the urge. Instead, carry one truth: strength is built daily. Not in grand declarations but in steady steps. One day. One choice. One breath.

You Are Stronger Than Yesterday

When you doubt yourself, remember this refrain: you are stronger than yesterday.

Stronger not because you never faltered, but because you learned. Stronger not because you avoided fear, but because you stepped forward anyway. Stronger not because the year was perfect, but because it was lived—fully, honestly, imperfectly.

Strength is rarely loud. It is quiet, persistent, steady. It is built in small acts, in repeated habits, in unseen choices. It is forged in resilience and tempered in gratitude. That is the strength you carry now.

And tomorrow, you will carry even more.

Final Reflection

A year is complete. Three hundred and sixty-five days of reflection, questions and action. You began with curiosity and commitment. You stayed steady when it was hard. You renewed, endured, focused and deepened. You practiced gratitude, showed courage and built resilience. Day by day, you became stronger than yesterday.

But remember: this is not the end. Growth doesn't stop because the calendar resets. What you've built here is not temporary—it is part of you now. Carry it forward into the next season, the next year, the next challenge.

You don't need to be perfect. You only need to keep moving forward—one step, one choice, one day at a time. That's how legacies are built. That's how lives are changed.

The story of this year is complete. The story of the next is about to begin. And you—you are ready.

About the Authors

Darren Gibbons & Alex Knowles are endurance athletes and performance coaches who believe that the strongest results come from the strongest mindset. With years of experience in triathlon, running and cycling, they have trained both their own bodies and the athletes they coach to push limits, endure setbacks and thrive under pressure.

Together, they founded Smart Performance Coaching (SPC) to help athletes unlock more than physical ability. Their philosophy is simple: without a resilient mind, training is incomplete. Endurance isn't only about finishing races — it's about building a life of focus, consistency and strength.

As athletes, Darren and Alex know what it means to face doubt, fatigue and setbacks. As coaches, they know how to guide others through them. Their mission is to build a community where mindset and training go hand in hand — where athletes don't just race stronger, but live stronger.

www.ingramcontent.com/pod-product-compliance
Lightning Source LLC
LaVergne TN
LVHW051727080426
835511LV00018B/2929